The John Clare S

The official Journal of th
published annually to reflect the
the life and work of the poet john Clare.

Editor
Simon Kövesi
(University of Glasgow)

Reviews Editor
Erin Lafford
(University of Oxford)

Advisory Board
Jonathan Bate (Arizona State University)
Gerard Carruthers (University of Glasgow)
Katey Castellano (James Madison University)
Paul Chirico (Fitzwilliam College, Cambridge)
Johanne Clare (George Brown College, Toronto)
Richard Cronin (University of Glasgow)
Paul Farley (Lancaster University)
John Gardner (Anglia Ruskin University)
John Goodridge (Nottingham Trent University)
Nick Groom (University of Macau)
Robert Heyes (John Clare Society)
Andrew Hodgson (University of Birmingham)
C. M. Jackson-Houlston (Oxford Brookes University)
Bridget Keegan (Creighton University, Omaha)
Peter Kitson (University of East Anglia)
Donna Landry (University of Kent)
Emma Mason (University of Warwick)
Scott McEathron (Southern Illinois University)
Jerome McGann (University of Virginia)
James McKusick (University of Missouri–Kansas City)
Nicholas Roe (University of St Andrews)
Adam Rounce (University of Nottingham)
Fiona Stafford (Somerville College, Oxford)
Sarah Zimmerman (Fordham University)

Number 41 July 2022

The John Clare Society

Patrons: Richard Mabey and
the Rt Revd Donald Allister, Bishop of Peterborough

President: Carry Akroyd

Past President: Ronald Blythe

Vice Presidents: Peter Cox, John Goodridge, Rodney Lines,
Kelsey Thornton

Chair: Valerie Pedlar **Vice-Chair and Journal Editor:** Simon Kövesi

Hon. Secretary and Festival Coordinator: Sue Holgate

Hon. Treasurer: Linda Curry

Newsletter Editor: Stephen Sullivan **Sales Officer:** David Smith
Archivist: Sam Ward **Publicity Officer:** Ann Marshall

Membership Secretary: Robert Heyes

Committee Members: Noel Crack,
Anna Kinnaird, Erin Lafford, Mavis Leverington,
and Mike Mecham

North American Representative: James McKusick

The John Clare Society is a UK Registered Charity, number 1124846

New members are always welcome; please contact Dr Robert Heyes,
53 Judd Road, Tonbridge, Kent, TN9 2NH
Email: bob.heyes@yahoo.co.uk

For journal submission details, please email or write to the Editor:
Professor Simon Kövesi, School of Critical Studies,
University of Glasgow, G12 8QQ, Scotland, simon.kovesi@glasgow.ac.uk.

© 2022 published by the John Clare Society
Printed by: Joshua Horgan, 246 Marston Road, Oxford OX3 0E
www.joshuahorgan.co.uk

ISBN 978-1-9161355-4-3

This is a limited edition of 500, free to full members of the Society,

£7.00 if purchased separately.

Contents

Editorial

This year's journal features a wide variety of critical takes on Clare, and shows just how many enticing and divergent routes into his world and work there are. Alex Broadhead returns for what is effectively the second part to his essay 'John Clare and the Northamptonshire Dialect: Rethinking Language and Place' in last year's issue, focusing this time on dialect – a widely-lauded but little-studied aspect of the poet's early experimentation. Robert Heyes – one of the journal's most prolific contributors – explores the world of the 'annuals' that Clare dipped into, those compendiums of literary and miscellaneous marvels that were so successful from the 1820s onwards. Bridget Keegan – another scholar whose work this journal has published many times – convincingly proposes the poetry of seventeenth-century literary pioneer Margaret Cavendish as an inspiring influence on Clare.

We welcome three new scholars to these pages too, forging fresh routes into Clare. Moinak Choudhury considers a feature of Clare's written work which is so common in oral storytelling: parataxis – which the *OED* defines as the 'placing of propositions or clauses one after another, without indicating by connecting words the relation (of coordination or subordination) between them'. In so doing, Choudhury offers a new theorisation of Clare's botanical eye and the poet's take on 'common sense'. Kazutake Kita uses innovative tools of systematic corpus analysis to assess whether Clare's sonnet writing is really quite as unique – formally, structurally – as many consider it to be. And Emma Nuding gives us some finely-detailed contexts in her histories of Crowland Abbey and St Guthlac, to help us better situate and understand some of Clare's most-loved local poems. Our annual bibliography of Clare publications will return next year.

The front cover features James Ward's drawing, 'A Wiltshire Peasant', *c.* 1811, courtesy of ©The Trustees of the British Museum. All rights reserved. On the back of the drawing Ward wrote that this was a sketch of 'A Man in Wiltshire who was in the habit of mowing two acres of grass per day'.

Simon Kövesi
University of Glasgow

John Clare's early experiments in dialect writing: the case of 'Love Epistles between Richard and Kate'[1]

Alex Broadhead

In this article I want to describe the behaviour of a lesser-spotted John Clare. It is the John Clare responsible for only a handful of poems among the great many collected in the Oxford edition of his works (1984–2003). Yet even in the context of those nine volumes, which brought many new sides of the author to public attention for the first time, these few poems stand out, due to their startlingly unusual appearance. In poems such as 'Lobin Clouts satirical sollilouquy on the times',[2] 'John Bumkins Lucy'[3] and, most of all, 'Love Epistles between Richard and Kate',[4] Clare experiments with punctuation and typography in a manner that is at once highly inventive, deeply suggestive and entirely uncharacteristic (when compared with his wider body of work). There is much that is not known about these poems: whether Clare considered them complete; what his hopes were for them; whether he submitted them to Taylor; why he didn't write more poems in this vein. The precise dating of these poems is also uncertain: Clare's Oxford editors draw them from the first Northampton Manuscript, which includes texts published between 1808 and 1819. For all that they are anomalous, and for all we do not know about them, however, I want to suggest that one poem in particular – 'Love Epistles between Richard and Kate' – offers us a new perspective from which to consider the role of language and literacy in Clare's wider body of work.

Historically, linguistic variation and, more specifically, Clare's use of non-standard spellings has been framed by scholars either as a proud statement of regional identity and political intent or, alternatively, as symptomatic of his limited schooling.[5] But I argue the language of 'Love Epistles between Richard and Kate' is concerned with neither. Instead it reveals Clare experimenting with spelling in order to explore the often problematic ways in which social status, education and gender difference intersected in labouring-class communities. In other, similar poems, however – in particular 'Lobin Clouts satirical sollilouquy on the times' – we find Clare putting spelling variation to different use, in order to put distance between the speaker of the poem and the employers whose treatment he protests. Considered together, what the two texts bring to light is a poet for whom linguistic variation is a source of both social complexity and rich artistic possibility.

It is remarkable that these texts, like a handful of others from the same period and written in a similar style, stayed out of print for so long and that they have attracted comparatively little scholarly attention. An essay by Stephen Colclough, published in 2000, constitutes one exception to this tendency, observing of poems including 'Lobin Clouts satirical sollilouquy on the times' that 'in using dialect Clare is experimenting with the accepted ways of presenting a working-place voice'.[6] Another can be found in John Barrell's review of *The Early Poems of John Clare: 1804-1822*, in which he observes that the uncovering of 'poems and songs written wholly in dialect' give the impression of 'quite a new poet'.[7] Barrell singles out 'Love Epistles between Richard and Kate' for comment, and notes (perhaps prompted by Clare's use of macrons) that it employs 'material and verse-forms which seem to anticipate William Barnes'.[8] 'Love Epistles between Richard and Kate' is also included by Simon Kövesi in a list of Clare's early poems on women which give rise to 'complex textual and interpretative issues'.[9]

These poems offer a marked contrast to Clare's wider body of work both in the density of their dialect representation and the orthographical inventiveness with which Clare renders local speech sounds. Because of this, they shed important light on Clare's approach to dialect writing and constitute rare and remarkable written evidence of historical pronunciations that would otherwise not exist. It is to poems such as these that Clare's Oxford editors refer when they invite us to:

> Consider the dialect-poetry represented here. In most of Clare's poems already published he is not a dialect-poet and does not intend to be one. Odd words or phrases from his Helpston vocabulary are glossed in his early published volumes, rusticisms of grammar occasionally evade John Taylor's eye, and later editors or biographers may have occasionally referred to a true dialect-poem, but, in general, Clare's dialect-poetry is still unknown. The omission of it creates a very misleading picture of Clare [...] [These poems] reveal

Clare as hard-headed, reeking of the farm, well-acquainted with village morals or the lack of them, and capable of self-ridicule.[10]

For Clare's editors, these long-hidden texts are self-evidently instances of 'dialect-poetry'. It is odd, therefore, that they do not linger at all on what is most immediately and obviously different about them: namely, the dialect itself, and the remarkably idiosyncratic and inventive orthographical strategies Clare employs to represent pronunciations. As this article will suggest, behind the rustic persona that Clare's editors conflate with the poet is an author and a sociolinguist carefully listening for nuanced differences of sound and imaginatively exploring the social meanings attached to them. Through a detailed linguistic analysis of Clare's spellings in 'Love Epistles between Richard and Kate' and 'Lobin Clouts satirical sollilouquy on the times', cross-referenced against accounts of phonology in Northamptonshire, I aim to describe a poet who is not so much 'hard-headed' as sharp-eared. What is more, the poem reveals Clare to be a shrewd commentator on the ambivalent ways in which literacy was transforming social reality for the agricultural labouring class.

Clare's editors describe poems such as the 'Love Epistles' as 'dialect-poetry' and distinguish them from other productions which make use of non-standard language. From a cursory glance at the 'Love Epistles', for instance, it is not difficult to see why:

> For ere I 'rit this scraūling let'er
> (I wish I coul'd ha' 'rit a bet'er)
> Fe'ēring sūm peeping chaps mi''te 'no'
> I 'new not 'ardly w'ere to go (ll. 41-4)

In contrast with Clare's tendency to avoid punctuation in his better-known manuscript poetry, the lines of this stanza are loaded with macrons and apostrophes, in one case two in immediate succession. Jane Hodson notes that 'apostrophes are used by authors to indicate that letters have been omitted on purpose rather than as a typographical error'.[11] Here, as in other, similar poems, the presence of apostrophes serves unmistakeably to frame Clare's language as part of an attempt to invoke particular ways of talking and writing, and particular social identities associated with those ways of talking and writing. In a later study of dialect representation in the Romantic period, Hodson notes that 'it is simply not possible to determine exactly which features of his non-standard language Clare intended to achieve a "deliberate effect"'.[12] Hodson's caution offers a balancing counterpoint to those readings which have tended to overstate the political significance of Clare's language in his wider body of work. But, in this context at least, it is evident that non-standard language is being employed with purpose. This is dialect poetry in that it has explicit things to say about dialect, unlike the great majority of Clare's more famous works.

And yet the 'dialect poetry' label requires some qualification. Graham Shorrocks offers the following, oft-cited definition of dialect literature:

> works composed wholly (sometimes partly) in a non-standard dialect, and aimed essentially, though not exclusively, at a non-standard-dialect-speaking readership.[13]

There are different ways in which a text might be targeted at a particular readership. As Patrick Honeybone has suggested, the orientation of dialect literature towards a specific (local, dialect-speaking) readership is often inferable from dialect writers' spellings, which frequently call on the insider 'knowledge of the reader to fill in the details'.[14] Elsewhere, I have argued that dialect literature as a mode took several decades to develop into the form described by Shorrocks (as late as the mid-nineteenth century, in fact).[15] Earlier works composed largely in non-standard dialect were, more often than not, mediated for general, non-speakers of the dialect through complex paratextual apparatuses, such as glossaries, footnotes and prefaces.[16] Regardless, what seems to be crucial in any definition of dialect literature is the relationship between writer, text and reader. This relationship might arise from an author or publisher creating and distributing the texts for a specific geographically-defined audience. Alternatively, the relationship might be suggested by writers employing spellings which presuppose that readers will connect them with ideas about how local people talk. Likewise, a relationship might be established by a writer or editor framing the text with paratexts which mediate the local content for a specific audience (be it regional or national).

If these texts can be classed as dialect literature, then it is in spite of the fact that they are not ostensibly aimed at a 'non-standard-dialect-speaking readership'. We do not know for whom or what they were written. And, perhaps more crucially, the problem with reading Clare as a dialect poet is that, for all of his oft-discussed acute sense of place, it is impossible to say precisely where his sense of the local, linguistically speaking, began and ended. One reason for this is that, as I have suggested elsewhere, the regional forms used by Clare had yet to coalesce into the idea of a single dialect. It was only in the wake of Clare's writing that this happened: his use of geographically-limited forms were employed by later commentators in order to bring the idea of the Northamptonshire dialect into being – an idea that was not available to Clare at the time his early poems were written.[17] The audience for Northamptonshire dialect poetry – the 'dialect-speaking readership' described by Shorrocks – did not exist at this time because there was no idea of Northamptonshire dialect with which the local reading public might identify itself, even if they recognised individual forms as broadly regional, in an uncircumscribed sort of way.

It may appear hair-splitting to debate the issue of whether or not these texts can be described as dialect literature. But I would like to suggest that recognising the ambivalent status of these texts as dialect writing is key to understanding what makes them unique. Unlike the forms of archetypal dialect literature described by Shorrocks, 'Love Epistles', along with other, similar poems of this period, is not a definitive attempt to represent a single, discrete dialect (be it of Northamptonshire, Helpston or the Midlands) but rather an experimental attempt to capture the speech sounds of Clare's local environment, and to draw out the meanings that linguistic variation – both in speech and writing – was increasingly beginning to carry in labouring-class communities.

In a later section of this article, I look in depth at the language used by Clare in 'Love Epistles' and 'Lobin Clout', paying particular attention to spelling. There are of course difficulties attendant on any attempt to analyse orthography in Clare's writing, in light of the generally inconsistent nature of his spellings (the reasons for which are discussed, for instance, by his Oxford editors[18]). In principle, this should mean that it is not always possible to know whether specific spellings are intentionally non-standard or (a separate matter) whether they reflect specific regional pronunciations. However, by attending to Clare's use of apostrophes and macrons, by looking for patterns and variation within the poems themselves (including instances of code-switching and reported speech), it possible to identify recurring, meaningful effects. And in order to uncover whether the spellings encode specific pronunciations, I have cross-referenced them against mid nineteenth-century accounts of

Northamptonshire phonology: specifically, Thomas Sternberg's *Dialect and Folklore of Northamptonshire* (1851) and Ann Baker's *Glossary of Northamptonshire Words and Phrases* (1854). In some cases I have also made use of a more recent account of the dialect, in the form of Mia Butler and Colin Eaton's *Learn Yersalf Northamptonshire* (1998), with the caveat that local pronunciations may have changed in the two centuries since Clare wrote these poems. To supplement these sources, I have drawn on more recent scholarship relating to linguistic variation in the eighteenth and nineteenth centuries more generally: namely, the work of Linda Mugglestone and Katie Wales. We will see, however, that while Clare's spellings assiduously record the sounds that he very likely heard spoken around him, they do not serve to perform regional identity, but are rather bound up with education and even gender.

'Love Epistles between Richard and Kate' is a pastoral dialogue between a 'Cuntry Clown' and a 'Milkmaid', as a struck-through subtitle in the manuscript explains, consisting of two verse letters in iambic tetrameter. Richard's letter, the first of the pair, expresses his love for Kate, complains about his own lack of skill as a writer and singer, and his reasons for keeping his feelings secret from his friends. Kate's reply offers no direct answer to Richard's protestation of love, but instead details her interactions with 'Farmers servant "Hobbs"', who delivered Richard's message. She describes her initial fear that the letter brought news of a bereavement, and her relief upon discovering that the seal was red, not black (which would have signified death). Following this, Kate reveals how Hobbs' attempts to reassure her fall flat after he reports that '"ther's nothing but good lũving in't"' (l. 104), which implies that he may already have broken the seal and read the letter. Kate's letter concludes with the couplet: 'Whats in't I says is nought to you / So I paid post and bid him go' (ll. 107-8). The abrupt ending of the poem, and the lack of any direct reply to Richard's romantic overtures, raises two possibilities. One possibility is that Clare had intended to write more, but abandoned the poem before it was finished. Another is that Kate's non-answer is the point of the poem: a bathetic, ironic but also fitting end to a poem that is consistently more interested in the anxieties and embarrassments of written communication than it is in love itself. Throughout the poem, it is not clear whether a relationship already exists between the two: Richard's letter makes reference to an earlier encounter, when he writes 'For ever since you jog'd from here / The day to me do's seem a year' (ll. 7-8), but the nature of the meeting is unclear.

The names of the characters hint at a source for Clare's poem: namely, Robert Bloomfield's 'Richard and Kate; or, Fair-Day. A Suffolk Ballad', which was first published in his 1802 collection, *Rural Tales*. Clare was a great admirer of Bloomfield's poem, commenting in a letter to Allan Cunningham that 'his "Broken Crutch," "Richard and Kate," &c. are inimitable and above praise'.[19] Bloomfield's ballad follows the titular Richard and Kate on their fortieth anniversary as they travel to meet their children and grandchildren on Fair Day, and share memories of their early courtship. Although the poem paints a picture of uncomplicated and idyllic domestic content, notwithstanding the 'pains and crosses' of agricultural labour (l. 126), the final stanza points ambivalently towards the impending mortality of the elderly couple, as 'the Sun sink[s] behind the grove' and the pair 'gain[...] once more their lowly rest' (ll. 151-2).[20] Scattered throughout the speech of Richard and, to a lesser degree, Kate (although she speaks considerably less) are a number of Suffolk dialect words, including 'mawther', which Bloomfield's editors gloss as 'a girl', and 'kedge', which they translate as 'Brisk, lively, in good spirits'.[21]

Clare's poem differs in several, significant regards from that of Bloomfield. In the first instance, Clare swaps Bloomfield's verse dialogue for an epistolary exchange and, in doing so, shifts the emphasis from the public and the spoken to the private and the written. David Fairer writes that the eighteenth-century verse epistle 'entangles private and public',[22] by virtue of the fact its appeal rests on the exposure of a personal, often intimate exchange in the presence of an anonymous reading audience. As noted previously, Clare's 'Love Epistles' were not published until nearly two centuries after they were written. Nevertheless, a theme of invaded privacy is central to the poem. Richard seeks out a hidden spot where he can write to Kate free from the prying eyes of 'peeping chaps', and Kate's letter expresses her consternation that 'Farmers servant "Hobbs"' – the man who delivers Richard's letter – comments on its contents. Here, as elsewhere in Clare's poem, literacy confers power ambivalently: it increases the opportunities for private communication, but it also increases the risk of being surveilled. Similarly, the ability to write carries with it prestige: Hobbs describes Richard as 'sūm' fine chap or ūther' (l. 105), presumably on the basis of his writing rather than his background. At the same

time, it exposes the writer to the judgement of others: a fact of which Richard is acutely aware, referring as he frequently and neurotically does to his own shortcomings as a writer of 'baddy stuf' (l. 66). At one point Richard refers to one of the 'boys', 'Jim', who apparently lacks 'sensē' and 'can reēd an' never spel'/ (An' 'rite a let'er mons'orous wel')' (l. 30). The use of 'an'' is somewhat ambiguous here: consistency dictates that Richard probably means to say that Jim cannot write a letter well, since he has also revealed that he lacks sense and cannot spell, which raises the question of why he did not write 'or' instead of 'an''. Regardless, in these lines we find the ideology of linguistic correctness leading Richard to assign different levels of worth to his peers, as he does to himself, according to their skill at writing and reading.

Clare was no stranger to the double-edged nature of education in a labouring-class context; Kövesi, for instance, has described the poet's belief that 'many [in Helpston] thought Clare's learning a "folly", and his scholarly habits "crazd" or even "criminal"'.[23] However, the ability to read and/or write was not especially unusual at this time. Martin Lyons, for instance, cites a study which estimates that, in England between 1760 and 1800, sixty percent of men and forty percent of women were literate, although he notes that 'bald figures' such as these 'say nothing at all about the quality of the literacy they measure'.[24] As might be expected, these figures were much lower among non-skilled labourers, especially in the countryside.[25] Even so, village schools such as the one Clare attended intermittently between the ages of five and eleven[26] increased the prevalence of literacy, such that 'in Britain and France, mass literacy was achieved by about 1880, before either country had fully established a system of free and compulsory primary education'.[27]

The ability to read and the somewhat rarer ability to write (the two were taught separately, as Lyons points out[28]) was increasingly becoming a feature of the lives of 'Cuntry Clowns' and 'Milkmaids', such as Richard and Kate, although not evenly, depending as it did on whether parents were able and willing to send their children to school. Clare's poem suggests that with that change came new, ambivalent configurations of power and status within labouring-class communities. The true artistry of 'Love Epistles' rests in its ability to convey this new reality not only through what characters say, but the subtle forms of linguistic variation that it sets in motion. Herein lies the final respect in which Clare's poem differs from Bloomfield's ballad: while Bloomfield employs dialect words selectively to evoke the overall Suffolk, labouring-class setting of the poem (as the subtitle makes clear), Clare uses dialect respellings to indicate not only differences in levels of literacy, but also nuances in the way that the characters perceive themselves and others.

Several cues in the poem indicate that the use of non-standard writing is not only intentional on Clare's part, but also a crucial part of its overall effect. In the first instance, the language of Richard's and Kate's letters, respectively, contrasts markedly. The first, written by Richard, features dense dialect representation, including clear attempts to convey information about regional pronunciation through the use of macrons and apostrophes. The second letter, written by Kate, tends to eschew these forms. Consider the linguistic differences between following stanzas, written by Richard and Kate, respectively:

> For ere I 'rit this scraūling let'er
> (I wish I cou'd ha' 'rit a bet'er)
> Fe'ēring sūm peeping chaps mi''te 'no'
> I 'new not 'ardly w'ere to go (ll. 41-5)

> For if the seal had not been red
> I shou'd have thought some friend were dead
> But soon the fancying terror fled,
> When I look'd on't and see it red (ll. 99-102)

Where Richard's verse is startling in its dense concentration of non-standard spellings and punctuation marks, Kate employs them much more sparingly. Most notably, the same words are realised differently by the two characters: Richard's <sūm'> and <ha'> form a marked contrast with Kate's <some> and <have>. This is not a simple opposition between a character who has mastered the standard and one who has not; the difference is more nuanced than that. Kate, like Richard, spells some words in the non-standard fashion and, like Richard, makes use of non-standard grammar: Richard has 'rit' (for *written*) while Kate, for instance, uses the uninflected form of *see* to mark the third-person past tense, as in 'He soon see me tho getting late' (ll. 85). As I argue below, Kate's letter features hyper correction, which indicates that Clare is consciously using linguistic variation not to mark social difference so much as satirise different social attitudes and self-perceptions. This is especially conspicuous when, at various points in Kate's letter, she reports the speech of Hobbs, a farmer's servant:

> His comeing thus supprisd me quite
> And set my very hair upright
> I'd like to faint; til he cry'd out
> 'Hoi dont be frighted I'm no scout'
> 'Ive sūmm̄ot here ya'l not refuse'
> 'Fūr if Im right its goodēr̄ news'
> Well more good news I says the better (ll. 87-94)

Hobbs' language is, in some respects, more markedly non-standard than Richard's. Richard's letter features some isolated non-standard lexis, in the form of 'gang' for 'go' (l. 15), and grammar, such as 'befel'' (l. 19) and 'rit' (l. 42) for the present perfect of 'befall' and 'write', respectively. But where Hobbs uses the second-person form 'yah' and 'goodēr̄' (for the comparative form of 'good'), Richard has 'you' and 'thou' (alternately) and 'bet'er' (l. 42). 'Yah', it should be added, is recorded in Baker's glossary.[29] What is significant here, however, is that Kate is code-switching to mark the difference, we may infer, that she perceives between her own speech and that of Hobbs. This is most apparent in the use of the macron, which Kate reserves for Hobbs, but also in the contrast between the two different realisations of the comparative of 'good': Hobbs' 'goodēr̄' and, in the line immediately following, Kate's 'better'. In Kate's decision to render Hobbs' speech as markedly different from her own, it may be seen that she, similar to Richard in his comments upon Jim's spelling, has internalised the ideology surrounding linguistic correctness. This in turn raises the possibility that Kate has judged Richard's writing efforts critically, as he had hoped she would not, and perhaps even that she has chosen not to reciprocate his romantic address for this very reason. The poem, of course, does not confirm Kate's feelings either way. Regardless, the epistles are shot throughout with a sense of the alienating effects of literacy and the hierarchies of correctness it presupposes.

Kate's greater proficiency at writing points indirectly to wider changes in female literacy that were taking place during the nineteenth century. Lyons, as has already been noted, observes that, in the late eighteenth century, 'sixty percent of men and forty percent of women were literate'. In one sense, Kate's aptitude at spelling belies this pattern. But on the other hand, female literacy rates in England had been rising, albeit slowly, between 1750 and 1840, as David Vincent observes.[30] Thereafter, the gap would close significantly, to the extent that women would even overtake men in the areas surrounding and south of Clare's home county.31 In the decades that 'Love Epistles' was most probably written (1808-1819), these 'rapid advancements' in female literacy had yet to gain momentum. Even so, the poem hints at a changing dynamic in gender relations: one in which a slowly increasing number of women were reading and writing. Richard's anxious response, at least, suggests that for some men this was not an entirely welcome development.

'Love Epistles between Richard and Kate' reveals Clare employing non-standard forms in order to create complex effects around social identity and perception, that extend far beyond any simple questions about Clare's own background. In contrast with Bloomfield's 'Suffolk ballad', regional identity does not seem to be important here: at no point do either of the characters make reference to a specific village or town, and there is no sense of where they hail from. At one point Kate refers to 'our Lee close', which, according to Clare's editors, refers to 'Ley Close, a small plot of land [in Helpstone] adjacent to Rice Wood (Royce Wood)'.[32] In a separate article, I draw on the arguments of the sociolinguist, Nikolas Coupland, who points out that 'even within local spaces, a sense of the local needs to be achieved – to be made socially meaningful'.[33] Put another way, the use of dialect need not in itself communicate anything about local or regional identity. Dialect must be framed as local, it needs to be actively connected to a particular regional identity, in order to signify place. When, throughout his wider body of work, Clare uses the non-standard expressions we now associate with Northamptonshire, it is overwhelmingly the case that he does not frame them in terms of local identity: when he frames them at all, it is in relation to class identity and social status.[34] Notwithstanding a brief and obscure reference to a local cul-de-sac, 'Love Epistles between Richard and Kate' is no different in that respect.

Even so, closer analysis of Clare's spelling choices suggests that, in some cases at least, he is attempting to render the speech sounds he is likely to have encountered in Helpston and the Northamptonshire area more generally. The remainder of this section focuses more closely on some of these spellings, before going on in the conclusion to explore their significance in relation to Clare's wider *oeuvre*. As noted above, it is Richard's letter and not Kate's which features the densest concentration of non-standard spellings. There is an undeniable incongruity in the fact that Richard's letter purports to represent the writing of a fictional character, and yet employs textual devices that are typically used to represent speech, as if Richard were both accidentally and yet very assiduously recording his own pronunciations. Richard's letter offers no indication that he himself is trying to represent a specific accent. On the contrary, he comments that 'I wish I cou'd ha' 'rit a bet'er' (l. 42), yet his use of apostrophes indicate that he is aware of the very spelling conventions he is breaking, which jars rather with his self-presentation as an poorly-lettered rustic. As illogical as this, it is no more so than many other instances of dialect representation, predicated as they are on the specious idea that Standard English spelling uncomplicatedly reflects Received Pronunciation, while other accents require non-standard spelling to reflect them accurately. Conveying sociolinguistic reality in writing requires conceits that don't stand up to much logical scrutiny, even if they help to make powerful statements about linguistic variation and how it is experienced.

Leaving this apparent inconsistency to one side, there is much in Richard's letter which is of dialectological significance, not least the profusive use of apostrophes and macrons, especially when considered in the context of Clare's wider *oeuvre*. Clare, as has already been observed, tended to eschew the use of punctuation in his manuscript poems. Consider the opening lines of the poem:

> Dear kate
>   Since I no longer can
> Go on in such a mopeing plan
> I send these lines with ham and hum
> To let the[e] 'no' I mean to cūm'
> Sūm' time or ūther you to see
> W'en things ar' fitting to agree (ll. 1-6)

In this instance, the apostrophe serves the conventional function of marking an elided letter, for example the absence of <k> and <w> in "no". In some cases, the elision of a letter communicates information about the sound of the word: elsewhere in the poem, for instance, *hardly*, *hanged* and *heart* are spelt, respectively, "ardly' (l. 44), "ang'd' (l. 51) and "art' (l. 75), corresponding to the general prevalence of <h> deletion that Baker observes at large in Northamptonshire speech.[35] Clare makes use of <d> deletion in his spelling of *and*, which is attested to in Sternberg's account of Northamptonshire phonology.[36] Another example of respelling unambiguously reflecting phonological differences can be found in Clare's omission of <a> from the beginnings of words, as in "pologin' (l. 69) for *apologising* and "bout' (l. 64) for *about* to reflect the deletion of /ə/ in pronunciation: a pattern which is, according to Baker, noticeable in Northamptonshire speech.[37]

In other instances, it is not clear whether the elision of a letter communicates information about the sound of the word or, alternatively, if it is an example of eye dialect: that is, a non-standard respelling which 'does not alter the pronunciation at all'.[38] Respellings which fall into this category include "no" (l. 43) for *know* (l. 43), 'mi"te' (l. 43) for *might* and 'wil" (l. 52) for *will*. In exploring the significations of eye dialect, Hodson cites Adamson[39] who suggests that it always produces a stigmatising effect, insofar as it implies illiteracy.[40] Certainly, this is consistent with Richard's repeated references to his own limitations as a writer, although it should be added that the poem is more reflective about the nature and effects of that stigma than is typical when writers use eye dialect. Hodson also notes that eye dialect may 'alert readers' to a regional accent, even if the spelling itself does not seem to convey 'phonological information'.[41] This is echoed by Honeybone who – to revisit a statement quoted earlier in the article – points out that words which appear to be eye dialect in RP 'can serve to direct attention to the word as different from their [RP] correspondents, relying on the knowledge of the reader to fill in the details'.[42] In this case, caution must be taken when discussing readerly inferences, as this poem was never published in Clare's lifetime. Nevertheless, Honeybone's observation raises the possibility that apparent examples of eye dialect arising from Clare's use of the apostrophe may in fact point to regional differences of pronunciation.

A strong case for reading some of Clare's spellings in this way can be made in those instances where historical changes to Received Pronunciation might cause a modern reader to wrongly identify one of Clare's respellings as eye dialect. Two such instances can be found in the line 'W'en things ar' fitting to agree' (l. 6): more specifically, 'w'en' and 'ar''. The substitution of 'ar'' for *are* may indicate that the word is to be sounded without post-vocalic /r/: a pronunciation that, as Mugglestone notes, was stigmatised in the pronouncing dictionaries of this period,[43] and thus was not considered a feature of the emerging prestige form of spoken English. Notably, Butler and Eaton suggest that post-vocalic /r/ was not spread evenly across Northamptonshire, in the late twentieth century at least:

> Northamptonshire people never roll an 'R', and as you will no doubt discover, deal with vowels in a very curious manner. The word 'for' is pronounced in the southern area in the style of the south-west dialect, the 'R' being produced with the tongue at the back of the mouth, which is called a "burr". In the northern area, however, it is pronounced 'fooer'.[44]

Clare hailed from the northern part of Northamptonshire, and his repeated respelling of 'for' as 'fo' in other poems of this kind, such as 'Lobin Clouts satirical sollilouquy on the times', provides evidence that, if he did not pronounce the word as 'fooer', he nevertheless did not sound the post-vocalic /r/ like those in the southern part of the county. It may be inferred, therefore, that the same is true of spellings such as 'ar'', 'pleasur'' (l. 38), 'wher'' (l. 55) and 'to'n' (l. 32) for *turn*.

Clare's tendency to delete <h> in wh-pronouns, such as 'w'en' (l. 4, l. 13), 'w'at' (l. 67) and 'w'y' (69,) can also be explained in historical terms. Mugglestone observes that:

throughout the nineteenth century [...] variation between [hw] and [w] in relevant words is, at least in theory, imbued with marked social correlations, demarcating "well bred" and "vulgar", "educated" and "ignorant" with seeming – if subjective – precision.[45]

Accounts of the Northamptonshire dialect do not make reference to the dropping of /h/ in wh-words as a feature specific to that variety. Whether Clare adopted the widely stigmatised feature to foreground Richard's low social status or, alternatively, modelled it on the speech of those around him is not clear. Either way, it is telling that Kate's reply to Richard, which is comparatively free of dialect features, features a gratuitous use of <h> in the respelling "Whi" (l. 94), for 'with'. This redundant <h> is suggestive of hypercorrection: that is, 'when speakers of a non-standard dialect attempt to use the standard dialect and "go too far", producing a version which does not appear in the standard', as David Crystal defines the term.[46] Such behaviour is consistent with Kate's characterisation in this letter: as noted above, the fact that she represents her own speech predominantly in Standard English but that of a farmer's servant using heavy dialect representation reveals much about her consciousness of social and linguistic difference.

Alongside apostrophes, Clare also, uncharacteristically, makes use of the macron in 'Love Epistles between Richard and Kate,' in such words as 'sūm' and 'ūther'. Esther K. Sheldon notes that, in a number of pronouncing dictionaries in the eighteenth century, this particular diacritic served the purpose of marking a long vowel,[47] as it does in the present day. In those cases where it sits above <u>, as in 'cūm' (l. 4), 'sūm' (l. 5), 'ūther' (l. 5) and 'dūn' (l. 40), however, the macron seems to perform a different function: namely, the pronunciation of <u> as /ʊ/ rather than the /ʌ/ of Received Pronunciation and the south of England. The regional distribution of these phonemes is famously supposed to distinguish the speech of Northern English from that of the South, and the isogloss which divides the two is commonly known as the 'FOOT-STRUT' split. Katie Wales, in her history of Northern English suggests that it runs along the southern county border of Northamptonshire,[48] which would suggest that Clare pronounced the vowel sound of 'strut' as /ʊ/, in the Northern fashion. It seems probable, therefore, that Clare's use of the macron above <u> is intended to signal this regional pronunciation.

Clare's use of the macron above <e> may indicate the lengthening of a long vowel into two separate syllables in the cases of *read* and *reason*, which are spelt 'reēd' (l. 29) and 'reēson' (l. 35), respectively. Sternberg observes of the Northamptonshire pronunciations of such words that –

> We also still preserve the original sound of the *ea*, thus – break, meat, mean, are pronounced as if written *bre-ak*, *me-at*, *me-an*: the pronunciation is better represented by the insertion of *y*, thus – *breyak*, *meyat*, &c.[49]

It may follow, therefore, that 'reēd' (l. 29) and 'reēson' (l. 35) should either be realised as /reɪjəd/ and /reɪjəzən̩/ or as /riːjəd/ and /riːjəzən̩/. The significance of other uses of the macron in the same poem, such as 'e'rēy' (l. 15) for 'every', 'ōny' (l. 38) for 'any' and 'scraūling' (l. 41) for 'scrawling', is less certain. But given the relative paucity of material on Northamptonshire phonology at the start of the nineteenth century, it is possible that these reflect experimental attempts on Clare's part to represent local pronunciations which were not attested in subsequent accounts of the Northamptonshire dialect.

In addition to the use of macrons and apostrophes, Clare in a few instances substitutes letters in a manner that corresponds to accounts of Northamptonshire phonology. The word *sorts* is spelt 'so'tes' in line 58, which presumably follows the same rule observed by Sternberg dictating that 'the broad sound of the *ou* in fought, brought, &c., becomes *o*, rendering them *fote*, *bote*, &c.'.[50] Likewise, *hang* is spelt 'hing', which is also recorded in Sternberg's glossary.[51] Other spellings, such as 'bōds' for *birds* (l. 58) and 'to'n' for *turn* (l. 32), suggestive of the substitution of /ɜː/ for /ɒ/, do not seem to be reflected in Baker or Sternberg, although similar spellings in Clare's other dialect writing, such as 'fost' (l. 30) for *first* in 'John Bumkins Lucy' do suggest that he was attempting to capture a recurring feature of local speech.

The picture that emerges from the narrative ironies and experimental spellings of 'Love Epistles' is of a writer with an acute sensitivity to nuances of linguistic difference, especially in the area of pronunciation, and the complex ways in which they are bound up with speakers' perceptions of others as well as themselves. Although there is not space to expand on this at length, a cursory analysis of other dialect poems, such as 'Lobin Clouts Satirical Sollilouquy on the Times' reveals yet another dimension of Clare's linguistic practice, both in terms of form and meaning. Where, in the 'Love Epistles', Clare favours apostrophes, macrons and letter deletions over letter substitutions, the opposite is true in 'Lobin Clouts Satirical

Sollilouquy on the Times', and indeed, a number of the respellings are consistent with accounts of Northamptonshire phonology. Respellings in 'Lobin Clout' which fall into this category include 'sich' (l. 4) for *such* and 'sarv'd' (l. 25) and 'desarv'd' (l. 26) for *served* and *deserved* respectively. Of the latter pattern, Baker observes: 'E is transmuted into a before r, and perhaps some other consonants, as "sarmon" for *sermon*, "parfect" for *perfect*'.[52] Other semi-phonetic respellings suggestive of Northamptonshire pronunciations include 'nothink' (l. 42),[53] 'chet' for *cheat* (l. 22),[54] and 'hod' (l. 5), 'that' (l. 16), 'os' (l. 28) and 'ot' (l. 38), for *had*, *that*, *as* and *at* respectively. This last pattern of respelling corresponds to a pattern in Northamptonshire phonology described by Baker as follows: 'the vowels *o* and *a* are often interchangeable, as *cotch*, catch, *starmy*, stormy, *ony*, any, *tromple*, trample, *crap*, crop, and many others'.[55]

A further contrast lies in the role that dialect plays in 'Lobin Clout': all but two lines of the poem consist of a spoken tirade against the exploitation and mistreatment of workers by their masters, as overheard by the narrator. Colclough suggests that dialect in this poem 'is used to focus the violent feelings of dissent felt by many labourers towards their employers'.[56] Certainly, the sociolinguistic concept of divergence seems relevant here in a way it is not in 'Love Epistles'. Divergence, according to Hodson, involves individuals switching 'the variety they use[] in order to increase the social and cultural distance between themselves and their audience'.[57] In this poem, it is as if Lobin Clout wants neither to be identified with nor understood by his Standard English-speaking superiors, and his dialect, combined with Clare's partial obscuring of words in lines such as 'D—n his old c-r-s (g-d forgive my s---)' (l. 9), helps to communicate that position. Correspondingly, issues of literacy, correctness and education are less important here than in 'Love Epistles' and this, at least in part, helps to explain the more sparing use of apostrophes in this poem as opposed to 'Love Epistles', bound up as they are in that poem with issues of stigma and incorrectness.

Notwithstanding their differences, the two poems hitherto discussed tell us much about Clare that is not apparent in his other, more famous writings. These poems represent provisional attempts to devise an orthography that adequately captures the linguistic differences to which Clare's life had exposed him, and to which his tremendous abilities had made him receptive. And, simultaneously, they are attempts to explore the literary and dramatic potential of the social meanings that were increasingly bound up with those linguistic differences. These are not poems about a place, even if the forms they employ were consciously drawn from the immediate vicinity in which Clare lived. These are poems about social and educational differences and attitudes, rendered in voices made all the more powerful by the fact that they are modelled on the voices that Clare had grown up hearing, and which he took such care to imagine into writing.

The contrasts between the two texts reveal a poet alive not only to phonological nuances, but to the different orthographical possibilities of representing them, and the ways that they can be made to mean on paper. They offer a powerful corrective to those readings of Clare which interpret his non-standard forms as a univocal symbol either of his background or his political stance. Dialect in these, lesser-known poems, is a focus both for virtuosic formal experimentation and detailed social observation. And yet the fact that Clare did not, in general, write in this mode is also instructive, reminding us that while Clare could think and write with tremendous intensity about the social meanings of linguistic variation, in most cases he made the conscious decision not to do so.

One explanation for this decision can be found in 'Love Epistles between Richard and Kate' itself. For Richard, knowledge of sociolinguistic difference brings with it anxiety and self-doubt; for Kate, it brings inauthenticity (in the form of hyper-correction), and, for both, it leads to an implicitly judgemental view of others. In this poem, Clare registers the personal and the social cost of attaching too much meaning to differences in the way that people talk and write. That he chose not to pay that price is further evidence, if it was needed, of his courage and independence as a poet.

Detail, 'Riverside Scene (Old Mill)', Peter De Wint, c. 1805–10, watercolour. Metropolitan Museum of Art, New York.

NOTES

1 The author expresses his thanks to the anonymous reviewer whose suggestions for revision improved this article considerably.

2 *Early Poems*, I, pp. 137-8.

3 *Early Poems*, I, pp. 196-7.

4 *Early Poems*, I, pp. 64-7.

5 See for instance Simon Kövesi on the linguistic debates underlying the 'editing wars' that have shaped the course of Clare's recent textual history, *John Clare: Nature, Criticism and History* (London: Palgrave Macmillan, 2017), pp. 127-40.

6 Stephen Colclough, '"Labour and Luxury": Clare's Lost Pastoral and the Importance of the Voice of Labour in the Early Poems', in *New Approaches*, pp. 77-92 (p. 83).

7 John Barrell, 'The Early Poems of John Clare: 1804-1822', *Modern Language Review*, 86.2 (1991), 411–413 (p. 412).

8 Barrell, 'The Early Poems of John Clare: 1804-1822', 412.

9 Kövesi, *John Clare: Nature, Criticism and History*, p. 206, n. 8.

10 Eric Robinson, David Powell and Margaret Grainger, 'Introduction' in *Early Poems*, I, pp. ix-xxiv (p. xii).

11 Jane Hodson, *Dialect in Film and Literature* (Basingstoke: Palgrave Macmillan, 2014), p. 98.

12 Jane Hodson, 'Literary Uses of Dialect', in *The Oxford Handbook of British Romanticism*, ed. by David Duff (Oxford: Oxford University Press, 2018), pp. 513-28 (pp. 522-3).

13 Graham Shorrocks, 'Non-Standard Dialect Literature and Popular Culture', in *Speech Past and Present: Studies in English Dialectology in Memory of Ossi Ihalainen*, ed. by Juhani Klemola, Merja Kyto and Matti Rissanen (Frankfurt am Main: Peter Lang, 1996), pp. 385-411 (p. 386).

14 Patrick Honeybone, 'Which phonological features get represented in dialect writing? Answers and questions from three types of Liverpool English texts', in *Dialect Writing and the North of England*, ed. by Patrick Honeybone and Warren Maguire (Edinburgh: Edinburgh University Press, 2020), pp. 211-42 (p. 219).

15 Alex Broadhead, 'The textual history of Josiah Relph's Cumberland poems: Inventing dialect literature in the long nineteenth century', in *Dialect and Literature in the Long Nineteenth Century*, ed. by Jane Hodson (Abingdon: Routledge, 2017), pp. 67-88 (p. 67).

16 Broadhead, 'The textual history of Josiah Relph's Cumberland poems', p. 67.

17 Alex Broadhead, 'John Clare and the Northamptonshire dialect: rethinking language and place', *JCSJ*, 39 (2021), 47-68.

18 Robinson, Powell and Grainger, 'Introduction', p. xxii.

19 To Allan Cunningham, 9 September 1824, *Letters*, pp. 302-3 (p. 302).

20 Robert Bloomfield, 'Richard and Kate; or, Fair-Day. A Suffolk Ballad' [1802], in *Selected Poems*, ed. by John Goodridge and John Lucas (Nottingham: Trent Editions, 1998), pp. 46-51.

21 Bloomfield, *Selected Poems*, p. 133, n. 45 and n. 94.

22 David Fairer, *English Poetry of the Eighteenth Century 1700-1789* (Abingdon: Routledge, 2013), p. 60.

23 Simon Kövesi, 'John Clare's deaths: poverty, education and poetry', in *New Essays on John Clare: Poetry, Culture and Community*, ed. by Simon

Kövesi and Scott McEathron (Cambridge: Cambridge University Press, 2015), pp. 146-66 (p. 146).
24   Martin Lyons, *A History of Reading and Writing in the Western World* (Basingstoke: Palgrave Macmillan, 2020), p. 90.
25   Lyons, *A History of Reading and Writing*, p. 94.
26   *Biography*, p. 23.
27   Lyons, *A History of Reading and Writing*, p. 94.
28   Lyons, *A History of Reading and Writing*, p. 91.
29   Anne Baker, *Glossary of Northamptonshire Words and Phrases* (London: John Russell Smith, 1854), p. 410.
30   David Vincent, *Literacy and Popular Culture: England 1850-1914* (Cambridge: Cambridge University Press, 1989), p. 24.
31   Vincent, *Literacy and Popular Culture: England 1850-1914*, pp. 24-5.
32   Robinson, Powell and Grainger, 'Explanatory Notes', in *Early Poems*, I, p. 566.
33   Nikolas Coupland, *Style: Language Variation and Identity* (Cambridge: Cambridge University Press, 2007), p. 121.
34   Broadhead, 'John Clare and the Northamptonshire dialect: rethinking language and place', p. 63.
35   Baker, *Glossary*, p. 300.
36   Thomas Sternberg, *The Dialect and Folk-Lore of Northamptonshire* (London: John Russell Smith, 1851), p. xiii.
37   Baker, *Glossary*, p. 1.
38   Hodson, *Dialect in Film and Literature*, p. 95.
39   Sylvia Adamson, 'Literary Language', in *The Cambridge History of the English Language Volume IV 1776-1997* (Cambridge: Cambridge University Press, 1998), pp. 589-692 (p. 600).
40   Hodson, *Dialect in Film and Literature*, pp. 95-6.
41   Hodson, *Dialect in Film and Literature*, p. 97.
42   Honeybone, 'Which phonological features get represented in dialect writing?', p. 219.
43   Linda Mugglestone, *Talking Proper: The Rise of Accent as a Social Symbol* (Cambridge: Cambridge University Press, 2003), p. 87.
44   Mia Butler and Colin Eaton, *Learn Yersalf Northamptonshire Dialect* (Dereham: Nostalgia Publications, 1998), p. 18.
45   Mugglestone, *Talking Proper*, p. 187.
46   David Crystal, *A Dictionary of Linguistics and Phonetics*, 6th edn (Oxford: Blackwell, 2008), p. 232.
47   Esther K. Sheldon, 'Pronouncing Systems in Eighteenth-Century Dictionaries', *Language*, 22.1 (1946), 27–41 (p. 32).
48   Katie Wales, *Northern English: A Cultural and Social History* (Cambridge: Cambridge University Press, 2006), p. 23.
49   Sternberg, *Dialect and Folk-Lore of Northamptonshire*, p. xii.
50   Sternberg, *Dialect and Folk-Lore of Northamptonshire*, p. xiii.
51   Sternberg, *Dialect and Folk-Lore of Northamptonshire*, p. 50.
52   Baker, *Glossary*, p. 2.
53   Butler and Eaton, *Learn Yersalf Northamptonshire*, p. 41.
54   Baker, *Glossary*, p. 2.
55   Baker, *Glossary*, p. 68.
56   Colclough, '"Labour and Luxury"', p. 84.
57   Hodson, *Dialect in Film and Literature*, p. 178.

Gazing on Guthlacian *Reliques*: John Clare's pilgrim-tourists and St Guthlac of Crowland

Emma Nuding

Scholars of John Clare have long viewed the poet as a writer deeply entwined with the landscapes around him.[1] However, long before Clare was walking, working and writing in such landscapes, they had their own textual histories, roving pilgrims and resident hermits. This is especially true of the fens – the low, flat and drained agricultural area just inland of the Wash on the east coast of England – an area on the edge of which Clare lived all his life. This article focuses on how Clare interacts with the legacy of the premier saint of that landscape, St Guthlac of Crowland (d. 714). Guthlacian content surfaces explicitly in two separate sonnets by Clare, composed between 1825 and 1837: one, entitled 'Crowland Abbey', and another, known by its first line 'Close by a lonely place that seems so lone' (hereafter, Clare's 'Guthlac's Stone' sonnet).[2] There are many factors which brought Clare and Guthlac into each other's fenland orbits: the reception of the *Life* of Guthlac in discourses around Clare; the work of antiquaries in restoring Guthlacian remains on the fenland horizon; and, above all, Clare's embeddedness within fenland networks, and his walking practice over its flat expanses, which undeniably put him within Guthlac's trajectory. This is especially true after Clare's move to Northborough in 1832, which placed him deeper into the fens, and deeper into Guthlac country. Despite moving closer to Guthlac and his *reliques*, the inaccessibility of Guthlac's narrative limited Clare's interaction with its finer details: for Clare and his readers, Guthlac remains a figure that is tantalisingly 'half erased'.

In this article, rather than the standard spelling of 'relics', I refer to an alternate spelling of *reliques* in order to point to the wider semantic range in the word's history. The word 'relic' has its origins in the Latin term *reliquiae* ('remains') which was borrowed into the medieval vernacular to refer to the bodily remains of a saint.[3] However, from the seventeenth century onwards, the term took on an additional antiquarian connotation, and began to refer to the textual or material remnants of past people or periods. The term is used as such in the title of Percy's *Reliques of Ancient English Poetry* (first published in 1765): on opening up this these volumes, the reader encounters not the relics of long-dead bodies, but the *reliques* of long-dead poets.[4] Published in successive new editions, the *Reliques* was read much by Clare and his contemporaries.[5] It is unsurprising therefore that Clare uses the term *relique* in Percy's textual sense: in his letters, he refers to a verse inscription left by the late poet Robert Bloomfield (1766-1823) on the wall of his summer house as a writerly 'relic' which one ought to go on 'pilgrimage' to.[6] Clare's use of the image of 'pilgrimage' to refer to visiting the physical remnants associated with a writer was not an uncommon discourse of his time, as Nicola J Watson has shown in her study on nineteenth-century literary tourism.[7] I would like to suggest that rather than responding to Guthlac's bodily remains, as a medieval pilgrim might do, Clare and his pilgrim-tourists respond to the fragments of Guthlac's legacy which remain in the fenland landscape, his *reliques* instead of his bodily relics. Like Bloomfield's *relique* on the wall of his summer house, Guthlacian writers too have left their narratives inscribed on the physical remnants associated with the saint, namely the remains of Crowland Abbey and a nearby standing monument known as Guthlac's Stone. In reading Clare's sonnets, we wait expectantly as pilgrim-tourists at these sites for Guthlac's shadow to flit between the columns.

For the readers of this journal, John Clare will need no introduction, but the same might not be true for St Guthlac of Crowland. According to Guthlac's eighth-century hagiographer, the saint started life as a warring Mercian prince, but ended up retreating to the island of Crowland in the fens, to live out his pilgrimage of life as a hermit.[8] These medieval fens, before major programs of drainage, were much wetter, boggier and (apparently) much more infested with demons than they were in Clare's time.[9] Despite such conditions, Guthlac persisted and established his hermitage. For the next fifteen years, he peaceably received many pilgrim-visitors, of both the human and non-human kind. After his death in 714, Guthlac's bodily relics were placed in an opulent shrine on the site of his hermitage, by the East Anglian King Æthelbald and administered by his sister, St Pega. By the eleventh century, the Benedictine abbey of Crowland was operating on what was thought to be the same site as Guthlac's earlier hermitage, and the monks invested in Guthlac's narratives through the commissioning of texts, manuscripts and carvings relating to them.[10] After the monastery was dissolved in 1539, the abbey church was left ruined and, later, it was partially restored as a parish church. For all of his life, the site of Crowland Abbey was within Clare's orbit: it was only a nine mile walk from his first family home in Helpston, and even closer to his home at Northborough, where he lived from 1832.

Haunting and majestic, it's no wonder that Crowland Abbey's ruins became the subject of many artistic treatments in the early nineteenth century, treatments which most likely influenced how Clare looked at the site. These treatments include an engraving by Hilkiah Burgess used as the frontispiece to the 1816 'digested' *History of Crowland Abbey* by Benjamin Holdich, which features a model viewer in the foreground, looking up in awe at the West Front of Crowland Abbey.[11] In the engraving, Crowland's ruins are overgrown with weeds. However, the West Front door stands ajar, inviting the viewer's gaze to linger on the dark interior.

Hilkiah Burgess (1775-1868), 'West View of Crowland Abbey, Lincolnshire', 1816. Engraving. From frontispiece to Holdich's *The History of Crowland Abbey*.

Treatments of Crowland in this picturesque tradition also include one influential depiction by John Sell Cotman painted in 1807 with a brooding storm cloud over Crowland's ruins on the flat horizon; they also include several drawings and engravings by Peter De Wint from a similar perspective, but in a more naturalistic treatment, made sometime before 1833.[12] De Wint in particular may have been a direct influence on Clare, as noted by Hugh Haughton.[13] Indeed, Clare was in correspondence with De Wint a year before the publication of 'Crowland Abbey'.[14] Clare even praised De Wint's depiction of the fenlands directly in a sonnet published in 1830, where De Wint's 'rushy flats' are said to rival more typically 'romantic' depictions of 'wild' skies, a phrase which brings to mind Cotman's sky over Crowland.[15] Thus, this artistic tradition of views of Crowland's ruins likely influenced the 'gaze' of the speaker in Clare's 'Crowland Abbey' sonnet.

Though Crowland Abbey caught the eye of many artists, it was not the only Guthlacian remnant on the fenland horizon which caught Clare's. There is a standing stone known as 'St Guthlac's' situated four miles north of Crowland along the Spalding Road, where Queen's Bank joins Wash Bank. The stone is about an eight mile walk from Northborough. Antiquarian Richard Gough recorded that the stone was renovated around 1750, presumably under the auspices of the Spalding's Gentlemen's Society.[16] According to the antiquarian Samuel Henry Miller, in 1878 the restored stone read 'aoi hanc petram guthlacus habet sibi metam', literally translated, 'I say this stone Guthlac has for himself [as] a boundary'; or, and more loosely translated, 'Guthlac has placed this stone as a boundary-mark'.[17] Given the inscription, William Stukeley thought that the stone marked 'a boundary of church lands'.[18] Present archaeological theory agrees with this assessment: David Stocker argues that the stone may have been one of several that originally marked the extent of the 'island' of Crowland around the twelfth century, and he and Paul Everson date the original inscription on palaeographic grounds to the late eleventh or twelfth centuries.[19]

We can confidently connect Clare's 'Guthlac's Stone' with this stone along the Spalding Road, restored in 1750. While there was a variety of boundary markers, standing stones and crosses around Crowland, only one known as 'Guthlac's' seems to have had an inscription on it in Clare's time.[20] A 1676 map suggests that at one point there was a second standing stone known as 'St Guthlac's' south of Crowland; however, by 1892, when recorded by antiquary

Samuel Henry Miller, 'St Guthlac's Cross at Brotherhouse, near Crowland', 1878. Engraving. Reproduced from *The Fenland, Past and Present*, p. 76.

A. S. Canham, this seems to have become known by the name 'Turketyl's Cross' and had no inscription.[21] The Guthlac's Stone along the Spalding road is also described as being in a 'garden' in 1892, which is also the setting for Clare's sonnet.[22] Therefore, given that Clare is responding to Guthlac's Stone on Spalding Road with the restored inscription, I would suggest that the restoration itself was one of the enabling factors which led to Clare's composition of the sonnet. The intriguing (if undecipherable) letter forms on the restored stone most likely furthered local interest in the story the monument had to tell in the century after restoration.

So while we have established that Clare encountered and responded to medieval remains in the fenland landscape, it is curious that scholars have not tended to investigate Clare as a writer who participated in the discourses of medievalism, a term which refers to the reception of medieval culture in the modern period. *The Oxford Handbook of Victorian Medievalism*, for example, despite having an introductory section on 'Romantic Period Medievalism', covering Blake, Wordsworth, Southey, Coleridge, Keats, Byron and Shelley, contains little reference to Clare or his work. The same can be said for Clare A Simmons' *Popular Medievalism in Romantic-Era*

Britain. [23] Though not under the lens of medievalism, the 'Crowland Abbey' sonnet has featured in a few select Clarean discourses: for example, the poem is featured in the on-site interpretation of the present-day Crowland Abbey. The poem also is briefly analysed by Sarah Houghton-Walker as an example of the depiction of the 'experience of sublimity when confronted with a sudden awareness of the past'.[24] However, the significance of Clare's interaction with the Crowland ruins has not been sufficiently explored, nor has 'Crowland Abbey' been analysed in conjunction with 'Guthlac's Stone'. Indeed, the 'Guthlac's Stone' sonnet has escaped the critical gaze almost entirely.[25] This critical gap on Clare's medievalism may be due to the tendency to view Clare as a naive nature poet, or 'Unlettered Rustic' with 'no advantages of education beyond others of his class' (a view propagated originally by Clare and his editor between 1818 and 1820).[26] However, this constructed image has been thoroughly dismantled by scholars such as Houghton-Walker, Paul Chirico and Mina Gorji, in their respective explorations of Clare's sophisticated religious reading, his interest in archaeological artefacts, and his intertextual allusion to Elizabethan verse.[27] I wish to take this revaluation of Clare further by exploring the extent of Clare's medievalism in a very specific case: the case of his interaction with Guthlacian *reliques* which dotted his fenland environment.

Thus, this essay tentatively positions Clare as a medievalist, albeit a somewhat frustrated one: Clare's correspondence suggests that he would have liked to be more immersed in medieval texts, but this desire was only partially fulfilled, stymied by his financial resources and the limited accessibility of medieval narratives. Clare declares in an 1826 letter that he wished he had access to a copy of George Ellis' *Specimens of English Poetry* (1801) and his request was repeated in subsequent letters.[28] If his attempts to get this text had met with success, he would have been reading a collection which included the Old English text of *The Battle of Brunanburh* poem with a facing-page translation, in addition to well-glossed texts in Middle English.[29] More happily, Percy's *Reliques* was one of the texts Clare managed to read, commenting that it was 'most pleasing'.[30] Though Percy's volumes contained few whole texts from earlier than the fifteenth century, the later ballads were framed as participating in a literary tradition which dated back to Guthlac's period. For example, in Percy's opening essay on 'The Ancient Minstrels,' which stretches from classical poets to Elizabethan ones, he postulates that 'the Minstrel was a regular and stated officer in the court of our Anglo-Saxon kings.'[31] Furthermore, an essay within the second volume of *Reliques*, 'On Alliterative Metre', included brief excerpts from Old English poetic texts, although Percy couples them with caveats about his lack of wider knowledge about the Old English poetic corpus (and therefore ultimately highlighting the inaccessibility of this early medieval textual heritage).[32] So while Clare's ambitions to read medieval poetry himself (especially early medieval poetry contemporary with Guthlac's *Life*) may have been stymied, we can conclude that medieval poetry as a partially-glimpsed but not-fully-grasped entity, did haunt his reading.

Aside from the question of whether Clare was or was not encountering for himself the poetry of Guthlac's time, what was the likelihood that Clare came across an account of Guthlac's *Life*? The text of Guthlac's eighth-century *Life* was published in 1783 by Gough, but this was without a English translation and in an expensive antiquarian volume with many plates and a limited print run, a format which ensured (whether by accident or design) that it kept within an elite readership.[33] Though the volumes were expensive, there were allusions to the *Life* of Guthlac in antiquarian writings in English, such as the second edition of Stukeley's *Itinerarium Curiosum* of 1776.[34] Embedded within a description of Crowland's ruins, and next to a 1724 engraving of the site, Stukeley includes a highly epitomised *Life* of Guthlac, tucked away in a relative clause:

> The abbey presents a majestic view of ruins; founded a thousand years ago, by Athelbald king of the Mercians, in a horrid silence of bogs and thorns; made eminent for the holy retirement of his chaplain Guthlac, who changed the gaieties of the court for the severities of an anchorite.[35]

Despite Clare's lack of funds with which to purchase antiquarian texts for himself, there is a chance that Clare might have had access to these antiquarian texts through his networks of friendship and patronage. Margaret Grainger and Gorji have argued that Clare had access to the library at Milton Hall, Peterborough, the seat of the Fitzwilliam family, through his friendship and correspondence with employees in the estate, including the house steward and archaeologist Edmund Tyrell Artis.[36] Clare's letters suggest that between 1825 and 1832 he discussed books with Artis, and specifically asked him for updates on his antiquarian pursuits,

John Harris (1693-1740), 'The Remains of Crowland Abbey', 1724. Engraving. Reproduced from Stukeley's *Itinerarium Curiosum*, plate facing p. 33.

while describing his own archaeological finds from his walks.[37] Indeed, Clare's move to Northborough was actually into a cottage garden owned by the Fitzwilliam estate, so he was arguably even more connected to the Fitzwilliam's and their library after 1832.[38] If the library at Milton Hall held volumes containing antiquarian descriptions of Crowland like Stukeley's, with embedded *Lives* of Guthlac, it is possible that such epitomes would have come within Clare's 'horizon of expectations,' to borrow a term from reception theory.[39]

There is a further form in which Clare might have come across details of Guthlac's life: the local Stamford publisher John Drakard published a 'digested' *History of Crowland Abbey* in 1816 by Benjamin Holdich, written in English.[40] Holdich's text was aimed at the 'curious' reader who wanted to know more about the ruins of Crowland Abbey but did not have an antiquarian's budget. Given its publication date, location, language and 'cheapness', it is possible that Clare came across this text himself, or perhaps heard about it through Artis. Holdich's *History* includes much more details from Guthlac's *Life* than would have been available in Stukeley's *Itinerarium*, including a two-page epitome translated from Gough.[41] However, despite this relative abundance of Guthlacian detail, Holdich's overall perspective on Guthlacian narratives is that they were impenetrable and confusing: he refers to Guthlac's literary tradition as a 'farrago', a 'jumble', something which is 'deformed' by 'contradictions and improbabilities'.[42] In addition, Holdich's own account is quite hard to follow, repeating as he does several different epitomes of Guthlac's *Life* at different points, and interspersing them with digressions: while Holdich reconstructs Crowland Abbey's narrative for his reader, Guthlac's own narrative seems to have only been partially 'digested'. Therefore, even if Clare did come across Holdich's *History*, his relationship with Guthlac's narratives might not have felt particularly illuminated by his reading; he would have come away with the sense that Guthlac's literary history was a 'jumble' and not a coherent narrative tradition that readers like him could access.

Unfortunately, Clare's Guthlacian poetry was written a couple of decades too early to be informed by full, accessible, translated editions of Guthlac's prose narratives. It was not until 1848 that an edition of the Old English prose translation of Guthlac's original Latin *vita*, with a parallel-facing translation in Modern English, became available for the general reader; this was followed six years later by the publication of a cheap English translation of Crowland Abbey's chronicle.[43] Even with these texts' low price points and high print runs, it is unlikely that Clare came across them: by 1848, Clare was a resident in the Northampton General Lunatic Asylum where he stayed until his death.[44] Though Clare had a wide variety of reading material in the asylum, he was physically restricted to Northampton and the immediate area, and presumably less well-connected to London's publishing networks than he had been. Poetic material relating to Guthlac took even longer to be published in accessible editions: extracts from the Middle English *South English Legendary* Guthlac poems were not published until 1881, and then in only an extremely limited print run in Walter Birch's *Memorials*.[45] Given Clare's interest in Guthlacian remnants in the landscape in the 1820s and 1830s, it is tantalising to think what he would have made of this hoard of Guthlacian textual material if it had (in some alternate universe) been available to him while composing 'Crowland Abbey' and 'Guthlac's Stone.'

Regardless of the accessibility of written Guthlacian texts in the 1820s and 1830s, it is likely that Clare came across references to Guthlac's *Life* in oral discourses, because of his embeddedness within fenland networks. While either at Helpston or Northborough, Clare lived about a fourteen or fifteen mile roundtrip away from either Crowland Abbey or Guthlac's Stone. Such a walk would have been within Clare's usual range: he was accustomed to spending whole days, particularly Sundays, out walking.[46] Indeed, Clare's notes record how in 1831, while living at Helpston, he spotted a 'large,' 'rare' bat while walking near Crowland.[47] Subscription lists of the 1830s also suggest that the rector of Crowland's parish church, along with other Crowlanders, were patrons of Clare's poetry, suggesting he might have had cause to ingratiate himself with the town's inhabitants.[48] Furthermore, Guthlacian traces in Clare's fens were not limited to the sites of Crowland and Guthlac's Stone: whether living at Helpston or Northborough, Clare was only ever living a few miles away from Market Deeping, whose medieval parish church is dedicated to St Guthlac.[49] Furthermore, Clare's journal also records him walking to Peakirk as an adult to collect ferns, and visiting his aunt there as a child.[50] The parish church of Peakirk is dedicated to Guthlac's sister, Pega; 'Peakirk' means simply 'Pega's Kirk' or 'Pega's Church'.[51] The relation between Guthlac and Pega, and Crowland and Peakirk, was presumably part of the local knowledge store, as well as being highlighted by texts like Holdich's *History*.[52]

Not only did Clare's embeddedness within these Guthlacian networks contribute to his exposure to the saint, but his walking practice itself likely made him more attuned to his environment, more able to notice and reflect on its histories, and on its eremitic and monastic ghosts. Recent scholarly analyses of Clare's work have explored how his walking practice enhanced his relationship with the non-human world.[53] As Robin Jarvis argues, walkers like Clare are enfolded in a 'flowing perceptual array' with objects growing in size in front of them, and disappearing into a vanishing point behind them, towards which they are free (unlike the driver of an automobile) to give a 'lingering gaze or a backward look'.[54] Such embodied experience means the walker is 'more alert to the multiplicity of appearances and the particularity of actual landscapes'.[55] In addition to fostering a greater intimacy with the non-human world, I would suggest that such an alertness also fosters meaningful interaction with the medieval *reliques* in the human one.

There is one specific aspect of the landscape of the fens that contributes to this awareness of the fenland walker: because of the flat expanses of the fens, vertical landmarks (such as spires, ruins and standing stones) can be seen from much farther off, compared with how they appear in a landscape with more varied gradients. This prominence of vertical markers in the flat landscape leads to them being used as orientation points in the wide expanses, giving feedback on the walker's location and progress. Clare was clearly aware of this phenomenon: his poetry repeats the motif of a walker stepping over a stile and gaining a glimpse of a church tower or other landmark.[56] For example, 'A Walk' (1832) describes a walk through the fens which is initially 'drear' but then reveals 'places rich to please'.[57] The poem describes the walk back as follows:

> —Now lanes without a guide post plainly tells
> Their homward paths— while from a stile is seen
> The open church tower & its little bells
> & chimneys low where peaceful quiet dwells.[58]

The implication here is that the church tower acts as a 'guide post', sticking vertically out of the land, from which the walker can orientate themselves to one of their 'homward paths' when returning from the wetlands. Thus, Clare's poetry shows that the flatness of the fens makes vertical points, even modest ones, visible from much farther away for the walker. Upright structures, like the ruins of Crowland Abbey, as well as more modest ones, such as Guthlac's Stone, become orientation points in the disarmingly wide horizon.

Reading Clare's wider poetry, therefore, we are reminded of the fenland walkers' increased awareness of landmarks standing vertically to the horizon. It is no wonder then, that in Clare's 'Crowland Abbey' and 'Guthlac's Stone' sonnets, the reader is provided with model fenland travellers who pause their journeys when they draw close to such landmarks. In their consideration of these Guthlacian remnants on the horizon, the travellers are prompted to meditate on the *reliques'* partially obfuscated histories. Indeed, in 'Crowland Abbey' the speaker invites the reader to share in their 'gaze' on the ruins of Crowland in the use of the inclusive first person:

> In sooth it seems right awful & sublime
> To gaze by moonlight on the shattered pile
> Of this old abbey struggling still with time
> The grey owl hooting from its rents the while
> & tottering stones as wakened by the sound
> Crumbling from arch & battlement around—

Urging dread echoes from the gloomy aisle
To sink more silent still—The very ground
In desolations garment doth appear—
The lapse of age & mystery profound—
We gaze on wrecks of ornamented stones
On tombs whose sculptures half erased appear
& rank weeds battering over human bones
Till even ones shadow seems to feel a fear.[59]

While 'Crowland Abbey' was first published in the *Literary Souvenir* for 1828, and included in both of Clare's self-planned anthologies, *The Midsummer Cushion* (prepared between 1831 and 1833 but unpublished in his lifetime) and *The Rural Muse* (published in 1835), Clare's journal suggests that the sonnet could have had its genesis as early as March 1825. At this time, Clare records reading an article in the Stamford Mercury describing stone from Crowland's ruins being dug up 'for the purpose of repairing the parish roads'.[60] Clare labelled those responsible 'modern Savages', and was clearly horrified by this utilitarian *spolia*, and its detrimental impact on the material remnants of the abbey.[61] Given the passion that the account aroused in him, he clearly had some personal attachment to the Crowland site and was invested in its material fabric and its histories. Clare's response may have even been informed by antiquarian discourses, either in his direct reading or second-hand through Artis: Stukeley's description of Crowland similarly laments how 'people now at pleasure dig up the monumental stones, and divide the holy shipwreck for their private uses'.[62] So while the 'Crowland Abbey' sonnet does not explicitly evoke Guthlac, or his narratives, the speaker can be read as a pilgrim-tourist who gazes on the ruins of the abbey, senses its lost grandeur and laments its lost narratives, as well as lamenting the dereliction of its fabric. However, this lament is clearly also pleasurable: gazing on Crowland's ruins is 'awful & sublime' because it makes the viewer consider how all past narratives, whether of dead individuals or dead institutions, eventually become 'shattered,' 'half erased' wrecks. Time, the great leveller, waits for no poet or saint.

Unlike 'Crowland Abbey', the 'Guthlac's Stone' sonnet does not seem to have been included in Clare's plans for publication, and was not published until 1995.[63] It was also written after Clare's move to Northborough, which, as Simon J White points out, brought Clare closer to areas of undrained fens, which stretched out from the new house to the north and the east.[64] Scholars have traditionally correlated Clare's move to Northborough with a decline in the vitality of his poetry: John Barrell sees 'disorientation' in Clare's Northborough poetry, a view which is echoed by Jonathan Bate, Clare's foremost biographer.[65] However, recent scholars such as Bridget Keegan, along with White, Gorji, Helen Pownall, and Simon Kövesi, have challenged this view, seeing Clare's Northborough poetry as not entirely evoking displacement, but evoking something much more nuanced, perhaps even an appreciation of the ecological richness of the fens.[66]

In addition to Clare's engagement with the ecological richness of the fens, I would suggest that the move to the fens also brought Clare closer to a rich source of poetic material, the 'half erased' narratives of St Guthlac. This is because this fenland landscape, fascinating and also sometimes 'drear', is the very landscape associated with the saint, from the earliest versions of his narrative to those contemporary with Clare: Stukeley's epitome, for example, describes the undrained fen around Guthlac's hermitage as a 'horrid silence of bogs and thorns', a phrase echoed in Holdich's *History* where the fen is deemed to be 'most horrid'.[67] Given such sources, it is possible that Clare was aware of the connection between Guthlac and the supposedly 'horrid' fen. Therefore, being in more frequent contact with such an environment might have brought the holy hermit to Clare's mind on his walks about the area, especially when walking past Guthlac's Stone on the Spalding Road.

Echoing this movement of Clare's along the Spalding Road, the 'stranger' in Clare's 'Guthlac's Stone' sonnet comes across a standing stone associated with the saint. This model pilgrim-tourist parallels the speaker of 'Crowland Abbey', inviting the reader by his example to meditate on the lost history of the *relique* in front of him, this time an 'ancient' stone rather than a 'shattered pile'. Despite the 'stranger's' intrigue, the 'pleasant man', a presiding local, can only partially tell the 'tale' of how the stone came to be there, because he 'cannot tell' the letters on the stone. Therefore, the 'stranger' must puzzle out the narrative of the place for himself by deciphering this *relique* from the past:

> Close by a lonely place that seems so lone
> There stands a house that nobody seems to own
> Yet there a pleasant man with much to say
> Lives & time passes pleasantly away
> The stranger often passes where he dwells
> & stops his horse & hears the tale he tells
> For in his garden which he calls his own
> There leans an ancient & a curious stone

The childern sit upon the stone & play
He tells his tale & never asks for pay
He calls the stone St Guthlacs now unknown
& cannot tell the letters on the stone
The stranger stands & wonders when he hears
& reads the story of a thousand years.[68]

The sonnet emphasises how vertical markers like Guthlac's Stone, visible far away on the fenland's flat horizon, call out to have their story 'told'. By the end of the sonnet, the stranger is apparently able to 'read' the stone's 'story', but details of this narrative are crucially withheld from the reader, placing them in the position of the 'pleasant man'. For the reader of this sonnet then, Guthlac's *Life* has been reduced even further than that of the Stukelian epitome, becoming a negative presence, an 'unknown'. While the letters spelling Guthlac's name (or at least the first line of letters 'GU[T]HLA') would have been clear to all literate wayfarers on the Spalding Road, the meaning of the whole inscription would have been only comprehensible to those like Stukeley with expertise in Latin and its abbreviations in inscription contexts. Thus by the end of the sonnet, we are intrigued by the stone's 'story', yet in the position of not being able to fully sound its depths: a position not so dissimilar to Clare as the frustrated medievalist.

'Combe Bottom', Sir Francis Seymour Haden, 1860, etching and drypoint.
Metropolitan Museum of Art, New York.

However, it may be that this tantalising frustration, the very inscrutability of the stone, is at the heart of its allure (and perhaps also the allure of other medieval *reliques* for Clare). The stone seems more 'ancient & curious' for being only partially legible and for withholding its full 'story' from most of its viewers. Joanne Parker's comments may be illuminating here, though her discussion refers to non-inscribed, prehistoric stones: she alludes to this dialectic between viewer and mysterious stone structure, saying that the very inscrutability of stone requires the viewer to bring to the stone 'as much, or more meaning as they find in them themselves'.[69] Indeed, in the words of Ann Radcliffe, in a poem published two years before Clare's 'Guthlac's Stone', prehistoric standing stones are 'sublime' because their 'purpose' is 'lost in the midnight of time'.[70]

Radcliffe's use of the term 'sublime,' as well as Clare's use of it in 'Crowland Abbey' is not surprising: Edmund Burke's *Philosophical Enquiry* (first published in 1757) influentially considered 'obscurity' to be a key component of inducing the sublime in a viewer.[71] According to Burke, an 'unfinished drawing' produces more 'delight' than a finished one, because when viewing the unfinished one 'the imagination is entertained with the promise of something more'.[72] Thus the ruined buildings and impenetrable inscriptions in Clare's sonnets, as well as Radcliffe's prehistoric stones, evoke the sublime in the viewer because of their obscurity, in both its visual and cognitive senses. Coincidentally, this rhetoric of obscurity is also something which medieval relic culture employs for similar purposes. As Cynthia Hahn explores, reliquaries are designed to partially obscure the relic within, making the relic all the more attractive, all the more tantalising, to the pilgrim viewer.[73] In contrast to 'Crowland Abbey', where we gaze with the speaker at the impenetrable silhouette of Crowland's ruins, in 'Guthlac's Stone' we watch from the side-lines as the stone piques the curiosity of the stranger. Before we realise it, our own curiosity is also not only piqued, but also pleasurably frustrated. Like the pilgrim in front of a reliquary, we have the sense that Guthlac's Stone could (if it only wanted) reveal to us 'something more', something tantalisingly out of reach.

Since we have read the 'stranger' of 'Guthlac's Stone' as a pilgrim-tourist visiting Guthlac's *reliques*, we must ask what role in this scene is played by the 'pleasant man'. I would suggest that he can be read as an iteration of the hermit trope, a medievalist image which is in dialogue with Guthlac's eremitic practice in the fens.

The figure of the hermit emerges frequently in Clare's poetry, as Peter Cox has noted, often in reference to solitary fauna and flora, including primroses, sand martins and moorhens.[74] In a fen poem written after the move to Northborough, 'To the Snipe', Clare casts a wetland bird in the role of the fenland hermit: he describes the snipe's nest as 'mystic' because it is situated on a 'flag-hidden lake', separated from the world 'where pride & folly taunts', and so it is like an 'isle' in the ocean.[75] This image of a 'hidden' island-nest clearly has reverberations of medieval hermits in general, and Guthlac in particular. Clare might have been aware of such reverberations through texts like Holdich's *History*, which refers to the medieval 'island' of Crowland.[76] Unlike the snipe in her nest, or Guthlac in his hermitage, the 'pleasant man' in 'Guthlac's Stone' is not on a literal island surrounded by waters. However, his 'garden' is still a kind of island in being set apart from civilization, occupying as it does, a 'lonely spot that seems so lone', an eremitic wilderness updated for a Romantic audience. The associations between hermits in Clare's period and gardens, as noted by Cox and Peter Campbell, may also explain why this nineteenth-century hermit's island happens to be a 'garden', a secluded oasis set apart from society.[77] Indeed, the 'pleasant man' 'never asks for pay' and does not seem to have complete ownership of the land (he only 'calls' the garden 'his own', and 'nobody seems to own' the house itself). While this depiction may interact with the motif of the trespasser in Clare's poetry, as identified by John Goodridge and Kelsey Thornton, I would suggest that it is also in dialogue with the motif of the hermit, an ascetic figure who eschews conventional ideas of ownership.[78] The 'pleasant man' also receives pilgrims and wayfarers like a hermit would: Clare's stranger 'often passes' to hear what he has to say, and the localised 'childern' gravitate towards his hermitage, like the Orkney boys to a much later fictional hermit, St Toirdealbhach in T. H. White's *The Once and Future King* (1958).[79]

Perhaps significantly, there is no equivalent hermit figure to greet the pilgrim-tourist in 'Crowland Abbey'. *Apropos* of the abbey's desolate state (dissolved, cannonballed and ransacked for building materials) its hermit has fled the hermitage. Only a 'grey owl' presides. It is curious that while living at Helpston in 1828, Clare's speaker sees Crowland Abbey as desolate and uninhabited; after moving to Northborough in 1832, and moving closer to Guthlac, another Guthlacian remnant in the landscape is viewed quite differently: Guthlac's Stone becomes a living (if not entirely legible) monument to the saint, presided over by a dynamic hermit custodian, visited by curious pilgrim-tourists. From the perspective of Guthlacian studies, rather than being poetically deadening, Clare's move to Northborough in 1832 seems to have been poetically fruitful: a result of being pulled more deeply into Guthlac's orbit.

Far from being an 'Unlettered Rustic', Clare was a fenland dweller intrigued by the medieval remnants in the landscape around him and the stories they had to tell. Artistic interest in the ruins of Crowland Abbey, as well as antiquarian restoration of structures like Guthlac's Stone, likely attuned Clare's eye to the medieval remnants in the landscape around him. More importantly, however, Clare's own walking practice, his embeddedness in fenland networks, combined with the flatness of the fens themselves, contributed significantly to the poet's engagement with these *reliques*. Clare likely had some exposure to versions of the *Life* of Guthlac, even if severely epitomised in Stukeley or second-hand from friends like Artis, and knew of the saint's connection with the fenlands he moved closer to in 1832. Such influences likely informed the depiction of the 'pleasant man' as an iteration of the hermit trope in 'Guthlac's Stone'. However, despite Clare's potential knowledge of Guthlac's *Life*, the saint's main function in Clare's poetry is as a symbol of the obscurity of past narratives, rather than their legibility. Guthlac represents narratives which were once part of the common stock but whose contents now tantalisingly elude us. While Holdich sees the incomprehensibility of these past narratives as a negative, Clare's tendency to forefront what is 'half erased' or what 'cannot' be 'told' suggests that for him the medieval past's incomprehensibility is a major component of its attraction. Acting as true *reliques*, Guthlacian narratives in Clare's sonnets are all the more intriguing for being partially withheld, partially untouchable. Those who encounter Guthlac through Clare, whether they be readers or pilgrims, will be drawn to the sense of something hidden, 'something more'.

NOTES

1   See for example, John Barrell, *The Idea of Landscape and the Sense of Place, 1730-1840 : An Approach to the Poetry of John Clare* (London: Cambridge University Press, 1972); Mina Gorji, *John Clare and the Place of Poetry* (Liverpool University Press, 2008); Simon J. White, 'John Clare's Sonnets and the Northborough Fens', *JCSJ*, 28 (2009), 55-70 (107); Bridget Keegan, *British Labouring-Class Nature Poetry, 1730-1837* (Basingstoke: Palgrave Macmillan, 2008).

2   *Middle Period*, V, p. 312; *Middle Period*, IV, p. 172.

3   *OED*, 'relic'.

4   *Reliques of Ancient English Poetry*, ed. by Thomas Percy (London: Washbourne, 1857), pp. i-iii.

5   Thomas Percy, *Reliques of Ancient English Poetry*, 5th edn (London: F. C. and J Rivington, 1812); Thomas Percy, *Reliques of Ancient English Poetry*, 6th edn (London: Samuel Richards & Co., 1823); Thomas Percy, *Reliques of Ancient English Poetry*, new edn (London: L A Lewis, 1839); *By Himself*, p. 218.

6   *Letters*, p. 57.

7   Nicola J. Watson, *The Literary Tourist: Readers and Places in Romantic and Victorian Britain* (Houndmills: Palgrave Macmillian, 2006), p. 39.

8   Bertram Colgrave, *Felix's Life of Saint Guthlac* (Cambridge: Cambridge University, 1956).

9   Colgrave, pp. 20-1. On the draining of the fens see H. C. Darby, *The Changing Fenland* (Cambridge: Cambridge University Press, 1983).

10   'Houses of Benedictine Monks: The Abbey of Crowland', in *A History of the County of Lincoln*, vol 2, ed. by William Page (London: Victoria County History, 1906), pp. 105-18 <https://www.british-history.ac.uk/vch/lincs/vol2/pp105-118> [accessed 7 March 2022].

11   Benjamin Holdich, *The History of Crowland Abbey, Digested from the Materials Collected by Mr. Gough* (Stamford: J. Drakard, 1816), p. i.

12   Peter de Wint, *A Distant View of Crowland Abbey* (London: British Museum, 1784-1849) <https://www.britishmuseum.org/collection/object/P_1958-0712-343> [accessed 15 April 2022]; John Sell Cotman, *Drawing* (London: British Museum, 1807) <https://www.britishmuseum.org/collection/object/P_1859-0528-118> [accessed 15 April 2022].

13   *John Clare in Context*, pp. 54, 74.

14   *Letters*, pp. 61, 203-4.

15   *Middle Period*, IV, p. 198.

16   J. Roberts, 'An Inventory of Early Guthlac Materials', *Mediaeval Studies*, 32 (1970), 193-233 (p. 223); 'The History and Antiquities of Croyland-Abbey in the County of Lincolnshire', in *Biblioteca Topographica Britannica*, ed. by Richard Gough (London, 1783), XI, pp. 131-53.

17   Samuel Henry Miller and Sydney Barber Josiah Skertchly, *The Fenland, Past and Present* (Leach and Son, 1878), p. 76. The transcription and translation is by Miller.

18   William Stukeley, *Itinerarium Curiosum: Or, an Account of the Antiquities and Remarkable Curiosities in...Great Britain*, 2nd edn (London: Baker, 1776), p. 34.

19   David Stocker, 'The Early Church in Lincolnshire: A Study of Sites and Their Significance', in *Pre-Viking Lindsey*, ed. by Alan Vince, Lincoln Archaeological Studies, 1 (Lincoln, 1993), pp. 101-22 (p. 103); Paul Everson and David Stocker, 'Crowland 02 (St Guthlac Stone), Lincolnshire', *The Corpus of Anglo Saxon Stone Sculpture*, <https://chacklepie.com/ascorpus/catvol5.php?pageNum_urls=113&totalRows_urls=369> [accessed 8 May 2022].

20   A. S. Canham, 'Notes on the History, Charters, and Ancient Crosses of Crowland', *Fenland Notes and Queries*, 2 (1892), 236-52 (p. 246).

21   Michael Chisholm, *In the Shadow of the Abbey Crowland* (Coleford: Douglas McLean, 2013), fig. 3.1; Canham, p. 237.

22   Canham, p. 247.

23 *The Oxford Handbook of Victorian Medievalism*, (Oxford University Press, 2020); Clare A. Simmons, *Popular Medievalism in Romantic-Era Britain*, Nineteenth-Century Major Lives and Letters (Basingstoke: Palgrave Macmillan, 2011).

24 Sarah Houghton-Walker, *John Clare's Religion* (Farnham: Ashgate, 2009), p. 166.

25 I am grateful that the 'Guthlac's Stone' sonnet was first brought to my attention by a blog post by J. Johnson Smith, 'John Clare, Guthlac and Croyland', 2018 <https://poetryparc.wordpress.com/2018/12/25/john-clare-guthlac-and-croyland/> [accessed 12 February 2021].

26 *Critical Heritage*, pp. 29, 42. Also see David Perkins, 'Sweet Helpston! John Clare on Badger Baiting', *Studies in Romanticism*, 38.3 (1999), 387-407 (p. 395).

27 Houghton-Walker, pp. 1-2, 85; Paul Chirico, *John Clare and the Imagination of the Reader* (Basingstoke: Palgrave Macmillan, 2007), pp. 78-96; Gorji, *John Clare and the Place of Poetry*, pp. 1-15, 77-96.

28 *Letters*, pp. 193, 195-6.

29 George Ellis, *Specimens of the Early English Poets* (London: Nicol, 1803), pp. 14-35, 65.

30 *Letters*, p. 57.

31 Percy, I, pp. xxv-lxi, xxxiii.

32 Percy, II, pp. 285-301, 286-7.

33 Gough, XI. On the prohibitive costs of antiquarian publications see Rosemary Sweet, *Antiquaries: The Discovery of the Past in Eighteenth-Century Britain* (London: Hambledon and London, 2004), p. 32.

34 Stukeley, pp. 33-4.

35 Stukeley, pp. 33-4.

36 *Natural History*, pp. 168-9, appendix Vc;. Mina Gorji, 'John Clare and the Language of Listening', *Romanticism*, 26.2 (2020), 153-67 (n. 25).

37 *Letters*, pp. 168, 264-5.

38 *Biography*, pp. 361-2.

39 Hans Robert Jauss, 'Literary History as a Challenge to Literary Theory', trans. by Elizabeth Benzinger, *New Literary History*, 2.1 (1970), 7-37.

40 Holdich, pp. iii, vi, vii.

41 Holdich, pp. 21-3.

42 Holdich, pp. 6, 10, 21-3.

43 Charles Wycliffe Goodwin, *The Anglo-Saxon Version of the Life of St. Guthlac, Hermit of Crowland.* (London, 1848); *Ingulph's Chronicle of the Abbey of Croyland*, trans. by H. T. Riley, Bohn's Antiquarian Library (London: G. Bell, reprinted 1908).

44 *Biography*, pp. 465-85.

45 Walter de Gray Birch, *Memorials of Saint Guthlac of Crowland* (Wisbech: Leach, 1881).

46 *By Himself*, pp. 32, 40-1.

47 *Natural History*, p. 79.

48 *Middle Period*, III, pp. xxii, xxxv, xxxiv.

49 *By Himself*, pp. 103-4.

50 *Natural History*, pp. 89, 203; White, p. 55.

51 *Key to English Place Names*, 'Peakirk'.

52 Holdich, pp. 27-8.

53   Robin Jarvis, *Romantic Writing and Pedestrian Travel* (Palgrave Macmillan,1997), pp. 67-70; Lance Newman, 'John Clare, Henry David Thoreau, and Walking', *JCSJ*, 34 (2015), 51-62, (95); Anne D. Wallace, *Walking, Literature, and English Culture: The Origins and Uses of Peripatetic in the Nineteenth Century* (Oxford University Press, 1994); Thomas Bristow, 'Decolonized Pastoral: Perambulatory Perception and the Locus of Loss', *Nineteenth-Century Contexts*, 41.1 (2019), 35-49.

54   Jarvis, p. 68.

55   Jarvis, pp. 68-9.

56   *Midsummer Cushion*, pp. 415, 428.

57   *Middle Period*, IV, pp. 311-13.

58   *Middle Period*, IV, pp. 312.

59   *Middle Period*, IV, p. 172.

60   *By Himself*, pp. xi, 172, 216; *Middle Period*, IV, p. 598.

61   *By Himself*, p. 216.

62   Stukeley, p. 33.

63   *Northborough Sonnets*, p. 97.

64   White, p. 56.

65   Barrell, pp. 174-80; *Biography*, p. 404.

66   White, p. 55; Helen Pownall, 'Syntax and World-View in John Clare's Fen Poems', *JCSJ*, 34 (2015), 37-50, 95; Keegan and James C. McKusick, 'Learning to Love the Fens: An Introduction to Romanticism, Ecology, and Pedagogy' <https://romantic-circles.org/pedagogies/commons/ecology/mckusickkeegan/mckusickkeegan.html> [accessed 1 February 2021]; Keegan, *British Labouring-Class Nature Poetry*, pp. 148-70; Gorji, *John Clare and the Place of Poetry*, pp. 97-121; Simon Kövesi, *John Clare: Nature, Criticism and History* (London: Palgrave Macmillan, 2017), p. 30.

67   Stukeley, p. 34; Holdich, pp. 1-9, 17.

68   *Middle Period*, V, p. 312.

69   *Written on Stone: The Cultural Reception of British Prehistoric Monuments*, ed. by Joanne Parker (Cambridge: Cambridge Scholars Publishing, 2009), pp. 1, 51.

70   Parker, p. 52; Ann Ward Radcliffe, 'Salisbury Plains: Stonehenge', in *Gaston de Blondville and St Alban's Abbey* (London: Colburn, 1826), p. 109.

71   Edmund Burke, *A Philosophical Enquiry into the Origin of Our Ideas of the Sublime and Beautiful*, ed. by James T. Boulton (London: Routledge, 1958), pp. 58-9.

72   Burke, p. 77.

73   Cynthia Hahn, *The Reliquary Effect: Enshrining the Sacred Object* (London: Reaktion, 2017), p. 37.

74   Peter Cox, '"From the World Away": Clare and the Hermit's Life', *JCSJ*, 36 (2017), 17-30 (90); *Midsummer Cushion*, pp. 432, 460, 467.

75   *Middle Period*, IV, pp. 574-77.

76   Holdich, pp. 1-3.

77   Gordon Campbell, *The Hermit in the Garden: From Imperial Rome to Ornamental Gnome* (Oxford: Oxford University Press, 2013), p. 29; Cox, pp. 432, 460, 467.

78   *John Clare in Context*, pp. 90-1.

79   T. H. White, *The Once and Future King* (London: Collins, 1958).

Speaking for Trees:
An Argument for Margaret Cavendish's Influence on John Clare

Bridget Keegan

The influence of seventeenth-century writers on John Clare's poetry is well documented. Mina Gorji, John Goodridge, and others have deepened our appreciation for the richness of Clare's engagement with a group he identified as the 'the old poets'.[1] While there is no question that Clare read, imitated, and even impersonated Izaak Walton, William Davenant, and Andrew Marvell among others, in this essay I propose that a less well-known seventeenth-century poet might have influenced Clare, and, moreover, influenced some of his most powerful poetry about nature, including one of his most stylistically ambitious poems of eco-protest: 'The Lament of Swordy Well'. That poet is Margaret Cavendish, Duchess of Newcastle.

There is no direct evidence that Clare owned any books or anthologies containing Cavendish's writing; however, given what we know of Clare's voracious reading habits and his broad network of fellow readers who made works available to him, I believe I can identify at least one credible avenue for Clare to have encountered Cavendish. And, although Clare never explicitly mentions her or her work by name in his own writing, there are several clues that indicate he may have had a familiarity with Cavendish's distinctive style and subject matter. Admittedly, the connections proposed here are suggestive only and would require additional archival research to be confirmed. Proving such a connection would enrich our understanding of the originality and complexity of Clare's writing about nature, of the depth of his engagement with literary tradition and with women writers, in particular, and of the impact of his intellectual connections with his contemporaries, most notably with Charles Lamb.

By way of background, my suspicions regarding a Clare-Cavendish connection began a quarter century ago, when fellow Clare scholar, James McKusick, and I began editorial work on a teaching anthology of British and American nature writing from 1600 to the present.[2] Because Cavendish is one of the most noteworthy early women writers about nature, she had an important place in the project, and I was able present her remarkable work in the context of the broader tradition of seventeenth and early eighteenth-century natural history.[3] I found provocative echoes of her themes and style in Clare's poetry. Moreover, I noted what seemed like intriguing parallels between the lives and interests of 'Mad Madge' and 'Mad John', not the least of which included their being labeled as 'mad' for their writing and ambitions. Although the social and historical distance between the two writers is admittedly great, neither had any formal education. Both pursued a passion for poetry, science, and natural history from outside of the mainstream (though Cavendish was the first—and for about 300 years the only—woman ever to be allowed into the Royal Academy). Both were criticized for the evidence of their self-education as well as their temerity in daring not just to write but to publish their work. Unlike the demurer aristocratic women poets of her age, Cavendish was a noblewoman who rejected the confines of manuscript and coterie circulation of her work. Clare was a rural laborer who aspired to be more than a mute inglorious Milton. Perhaps the most intriguing, and the strongest argument for influence, is that both demonstrated a level of ecological awareness and struggled to resist anthropocentric techniques for representing nature, adopting original if imperfect strategies in their poetry to give nature a voice—and a voice that is more authentically nature's own. The poet Alice Fulton has also remarked upon the similarities between the two writers, describing how their poems 'suggest sympathetic connections between human and animal intelligences'.[4]

Informed by her unique scientific worldview, Cavendish wrote poems about the natural world that exhibited an environmental ethos that seems presciently modern. For example, her 'A Dialogue Between An Oak, and a Man Cutting Him Down' opens with the Oak enumerating all the benefits he has provided to man, from meeting his practical needs like shelter to offering him aesthetic pleasures by giving the birds a place to sing.[5] Planning to use the oak's wood to build a ship, the man looks to the abundance of acorns ready to replace the fully matured tree as a justification for his destructive actions. Cavendish thus explicitly links deforestation with colonial ambitions. The oak protests:

> I care not for that wealth, wherein the pains,
> And troubles are far greater than the gains.
> I am contented with what Nature gave;
> I'd not repine, but one poor wish would have,
> Which is, that you my aged life would save. (ll. 100-3)

The Oak and the man agree, however, on one thing, namely human nature. Humanity 'nothing loves but what he cannot get' (l. 138). Unquenchable human desire takes precedence over the conservation of natural resources.

Another poem, 'The Hunting of the Hare' details the pursuit of Poor Wat, from a perspective uniquely sympathetic to the animal and ending, again, with a critique of the human appetites that lead to cruelty and destruction. She writes:

> Yet man doth think himself so gentle, mild,
> When of all creatures he's most cruel, wild.
> And is so proud, thinks only he shall live,
> That God a godlike nature did him give,
> And that all creatures for his sake alone
> Were made, for him to tyrannize upon. (ll. 101-6)

These poems are but two examples of the many poems about nature included in Cavendish's collection *Poems and Fancies* (1653) that demonstrate an ecocentric perspective. Many of them represent trees, animals, or the earth itself speaking directly, whether in dialog with Man, or, more strikingly, directly to nature as in the powerful lament entitled 'Earth's Complaint' which begins:

> O Nature! Nature, hearken to my cry,
> Each Minute wounded am, but cannot die.
> My children, which I from my womb did bear,
> Do dig my sides, and all my bowels tear.
> They plow deep furrows in my very face,
> From torment I have neither time nor place.
> No other Element is so abused,
> Or by Mankind so cruelly is used. (ll. 1-8)

Ecocritics such as Ken Hiltner have demonstrated an environmentally sensitive perspective in the work of several canonical early modern writers, most notably John Milton.[6] What makes Cavendish distinctive among her contemporaries is her persistent use of the stylistic technique of giving non-human nature a voice. While one could make a case that these poems are not about nature per se, but allegories pertaining to court politics (comparable to, for instance, Dryden's *The Hind and the Panther*), I believe it is not anachronistic to argue that they may also stand as a protest against the human oppression of nature and the exploitation of natural resources. Such a view is supported by Cavendish's scientific and philosophical prose that engages the period's debates around vitalism. In her *Philosophical Letters* (1664), for instance, she asserts that 'sense and reason were present in all creatures, not only man and animals' – even going so far as to attribute life and knowledge to vegetables. As Donna Landry summarizes: 'The effect of Cavendish's argument is a democratization of relations between humans and other species, even between humans and other forms of matter – vegetables and minerals. There is certainly a basis here for an ecological non-instrumental relation to the natural world'.[7] Such a democratization of relations is everywhere apparent in Clare's nature poetry as well, as any number of his poems demonstrate.

Clare shares with Cavendish a thematic interest in representing a non-instrumental ethos in relation to nature. They also share stylistic techniques that enable them to achieve that goal. Like Cavendish, Clare experiments with ways of allowing nature to speak for itself, both directly and indirectly, as in poems like 'The Lamentation of Round Oak Waters', 'The Lament of Swordy Well', in his bird poems, or his several poems related to hunting, notably the Fox and Badger series. While Clare's 'To A Fallen Elm', for example, does not literally give the tree a voice in dialogue with the poet, as Cavendish does, Clare does claim of the tree:

> Thou ownd a language by which hearts are stirred
> Deeper than by the atribute of words
> Thine spoke a feeling known in every tongue
> Language of pity and the force of wrong
> What cant assumes what hypocrites will dare
> Speaks home to truth and shows it what they are (ll. 31-6)[8]

Like Cavendish's Oak, Clare condemns human greed that is 'thy ruin, music-making elm' (l. 65). Both Cavendish and Clare describe the tree as valuable not only as raw material for human use but also as a source of aesthetic pleasure, and both appear to elevate the importance of that pleasure beyond the tree's use value.

Cavendish and Clare's poetry about animals is equally interesting to compare. Donna Landry observes that Cavendish's poem 'The Hunting of the Hare' includes descriptions of the animal from the point of view of a 'field naturalist': 'Cavendish demonstrates an empathetic apprehension of the hare as a separate but fellow creature closely observed for his own being and behavior'.[9] The same comment can easily be made about Clare's poetry of pursued animals, most notably his sonnet sequence on the badger, which like Cavendish's poem, moves among perspectives, providing a lively narrative of the hunt as experienced by the dogs and men tracking the animal, the women and boys watching the event, and the badger itself. Cavendish and Clare's descriptions may be categorized as both 'scientific and empathetic'. They are accurate in their observations of the animal's behavior, but the human cruelty they both depict elicits an implicit, if powerful, critique of anthropocentric entitlement. Cavendish and Clare experiment in parallel ways to imagine what the voice of nature would sound like. Cavendish did not go as far as Clare to directly imitate bird song in her verse (as Clare does in 'The Progress of Rhyme', for instance) although she does have a lively dialog poem entitled 'A Parliament of Birds' that does not incorporate any human interlocutor, instead having the birds speak only amongst themselves, albeit in a human tongue.

Having non-human nature speak, for itself, in exclusion of a human voice apostrophizing it, is a technique that Clare effectively employs in 'The Lament of Swordy Well', a poem that David Simpson rightfully claims as one of Clare's most original. Simpson asserts that what is unique about the voice represented in the poem is that it is:

> not a tree, a spring, a rock or grotto, or a 'genius of the brook' like the voice of 'Lamentation of Round Oak Waters'. Not a nymph, a dryad, a cave or an oracular deep and gloomy breathing place. Not an animated tree that turns out to be an imprisoned soul, not a god disguised as a shower of rain, nor an eloquent wind scouring the surface of the earth. If none of these, then what?[10]

Simpson's response is that he can find 'no simple genre or rhetorical category that prefigures what Clare is doing here'.[11] The trope prosopopoeia may come closest in describing the technique. However, because Swordy Well is an imprecise site, one whose exact boundaries are not set and one that is comprised of an 'indefinitely describable series of other such [natural] objects – hedges, fields, springs, flowers, animals, trees, rocks, and so on and son on',[12] it is thus not a discrete object or singular 'thing' to which one can give face or voice, which would be the usual core characteristic of prosopopoeia. Simpson concludes that the poem is an example of 'Clare's extraordinary originality in giving voice to an unbounded place, thereby inventing a form of personification unrecorded in rhetorical theory'.[13] McKusick, likewise, remarks upon the poem's 'radical innovation' as 'one of the first and still one of the very few poems to speak for the Earth in such a direct and immediate way'.[14]

While not wishing to deny Clare's inventiveness, neither Simpson nor McKusick mention those poems of Cavendish where nature speaks, without or outside of human intercession. Cavendish also represents nature with a comparable boundlessness, as in the poem 'Earth's Complaint', quoted above. She does so again in another dialogue poem 'Nature calls a Counsel, which is Motion, Figure, Matter, and Life, to Advise about Making the World'. Although this appears to be a theoretical poem, one that does not emphasize descriptive details and conceptualizes nature as an abstraction not a physical place, Cavendish attempts to imagine nature entirely outside of human reference. The poem's conversation takes place before the creation of the world and therefore humans. She repeats this strategy in 'A Complaint of Water, Earth, and Air, against the Sun, by Way of Dialogue'. While she allegorizes the elements to engage in a scientific debate, she nonetheless does not directly involve 'Man' in these conversations. When she does, it is typically to place 'Man' in a negative light. For example, in 'Dialogue betwixt Man and Nature' nature defends herself again against man's rapaciousness:

> But men amongst themselves contract and make
> A bargain for my tree; that tree they take,
> Which cruelly they chop in pieces small,
> And form it has they please, then build withal.
> Although that tree by me was made to stand,
> Just as it grows, not to be cut by man. (ll. 21-6)

Nature here is a voice but not one embodied in the figure of a goddess, thus personified without necessarily being made into a person.

Finally, Cavendish uses poetry to ponder what beasts, birds, and fishes know and feel. In 'Of the Knowledge of Beasts' she wonders if beasts 'contemplations have upon the sun' (l. 3) and if they have the same curiosity about the heavens as humans. In 'Of Fishes' she wonders:

> Who knows, but fish which in the sea do live
> Can a good reason of its saltiness give,
> And how it ebbs and flows? Perchance they can
> Show reasons more than ever yet could man. (ll. 1-4)

Likewise, in 'Of Birds' Cavendish writes:

> Who knows, but Birds which under th'azure skies
> Do fly, know whence the blustering winds do rise?
> May know what thunder is, which no man knows,
> And what's a blazing star, or where it goes. (ll. 1-4)

Both poems suggest that non-human nature has knowledge, gained from an intimate experience of an environment that is inaccessible to humans. We see similar epistemological speculations in several of Clare's bird poems, such as 'To the Snipe' where the bird possesses a knowledge of the wetland ecosystem that is literally inaccessible to humans as 'The trembling grass / Quakes from the human foot / Nor bears the weight of man to let him pass' (ll. 5-7).

What makes Clare and Cavendish's poetry exceptional – and why I speculate upon potential influence – is their respective efforts to avoid easy personification and to imagine a consciousness, an intelligence, and a distinct voice present in nature, in animals, and even in plants. Their poems listen for a voice that is nature's own, refusing the anthropomorphic ventriloquism that we find in other Romantic period poets like Wordsworth and Shelley. Cavendish and Clare do not use figures like prosopopoeia to project their own voice onto nature—rather, as Simpson asserts, they aspire to work beyond the rhetorical techniques available to them.

Evocative as Cavendish's style may be in explaining Clare's, making this argument more than simply suggestive hinges on being able to demonstrate that Clare had read Cavendish's poetry. I believe this is at least likely if not certain. Where, however, would Clare have encountered Cavendish? There was an 1813 edition of her work, which was privately printed, with only 25 copies. Cavendish scholars note that the seventeenth-century editions were still in circulation in the early nineteenth-century and records exist of their sale. Were there original copies of *Poems and Fancies* that Clare might have seen in the libraries of Burghley House or Milton Hall? In terms of the anthologies that we know Clare read, and which were in his own library, the selections from Cavendish in *Poems by Eminent Ladies*, for instance, do not correspond to those poems that seem most strikingly like Clare's. Nevertheless, it establishes that Clare would have known about Cavendish in general. And we know Clare read and encountered far more anthologies and miscellanies than those actually in his possession. Mina Gorji describes how he gained familiarity with many of 'the old poets' from sources like William Hone's *Every Day Book* (1825) or the serial publication *Time's Telescope*. Additional library and archival work is needed to pursue these possible leads, surveying Cavendish's appearance in the popular poetry collections of the period.

By far the most likely connection between the two writers is Charles Lamb. As Mina Gorji, Scott McEathron, and Simon Kövesi have each separately written, a prime source of affinity between the two writers – and indeed, a source of cultural bonding among all of those affiliated with the *London Magazine* – was a passion for sixteenth- and seventeenth-century poetry.[15] Clare's sonnet to Lamb explicitly identifies this connection and opens with the following lines:

> Friend Lamb thou chusest well to love the lore
> Of our by gone bards whose racey page
> Rich mellowing Time made sweeter then before
> The blossom left for the long garnered store
> Of fruitage now right luscious in its age (ll. 1-5)

Lamb had three seventeenth-century editions of Cavendish in his library: the *Works* (1664); *The World's Olio* (1671); and *Nature's Picture Drawn by Fancie's Pencil* (1656). *A Descriptive Catalogue of the Library of Charles Lamb* notes about these last two volumes that each 'bear[s] marks of careful reading with many marginal MS, notes, comments &c'.[16] Thus we know that Lamb had read Cavendish's work closely. We also know that he enjoyed it. Lamb was characteristically fulsome in his praise for Cavendish calling her: 'a dear favourite of mine, of the last century but one — the thrice noble, chaste and virtuous — but again somewhat fantastical and original-brained, generous Margaret Newcastle'.[17] Elsewhere he titled her 'that princely woman, the thrice noble Margaret Newcastle'[18]; and more intimately 'dear Margaret Newcastle'.[19] Clare visited Lamb's house at least once (and in the period before he wrote 'Lament of Swordy Well'), so it is possible that their conversation could have turned to Cavendish, and the opportunity might have presented itself for Clare to have read with Lamb or from the books in Lamb's library.

I recognize that my argument is full of 'might haves' and 'could haves'. Given that Clare was not afraid of naming his other early modern (or contemporary) influences, if indeed he had read Cavendish why did he chose not to mention it somewhere—if not in his poetry, then in his letters or other prose writings? He seemed happy to refer to other poets he knew and loved—especially those who would have confirmed the affinity of his taste with Lamb's. At the same time, Clare read very widely, and it may be that while he read Cavendish, she did not make a conscious impression on him, although the extent of the stylistic similarities makes it unlikely that the influence was 'unconscious'.

To be able to establish Cavendish's influence on Clare expands our understanding of Clare's debt to women writers, an area in Clare studies whose depths have only begun to be plumbed. Exploring the influence of seventeenth- or eighteenth-century women writers on Clare would complement the work that scholars like Emma Trehane have done on Clare's relationship with his patron Eliza Emmerson or that Clare Macdonald Shaw has initiated regarding Clare's connection to regional women poets like Anna Adcock.[20] That Clare's poetic voice might have been shaped by a woman poet who studied and loved nature as he did remains for now only a tantalizing possibility.

NOTES

1   Mina Gorji, 'Clare and Community: The 'Old Poets' and the *London Magazine*', in *New Approaches*, pp. 47-64. John Goodridge, '"Three cheers for mute ingloriousness"': Clare and eighteenth-century poetry', in his *John Clare and Community* (Cambridge: Cambridge University Press, 2013), pp. 36-58.

2   See *Literature and Nature: Four Centuries of Nature Writing*, ed. by Bridget Keegan and James C. McKusick (New Jersey: Prentice Hall, 2001).

3   See Sylvia Bowerbank, *Speaking for Nature: Women and Ecologies of Early Modern England* (Baltimore: Johns Hopkins University Press, 2004), and Bruce Boehrer, *Animal Characters: Nonhuman Beings in Early Modern Literature* (Philadelphia: University of Pennsylvania Press, 2010).

4   Alice Fulton, 'Unordinary Passions: Margaret Cavendish, the Duchess of Newcastle', in *Green Thoughts, Green Shades: Essays by Contemporary Poets on the Early Modern Lyric*, ed. by Jonathan F. S. Post (Berkeley: University of California Press, 2002), p. 200.

5   All quotations from Cavendish's poetry are taken from Liza Blake's digital, critical edition of *Poems and Fancies*: <https://library2.utm.utoronto.ca/poemsandfancies/> [accessed 1 June 2022].

6   *Renaissance Ecology: Imagining Eden in Milton's England* (Pittsburgh: Duquesne University Press, 2008) and *What Else is Pastoral: Renaissance Literature and the Environment* (Ithaca: Cornell University Press, 2011).

7   Donna Landry, 'Green Languages? Women Poets as Naturalists in 1653 and 1807' in *Forging Connections: Women's Poetry from the Renaissance to Romanticism*, ed. by Anne K. Mellor, Felicity Nussbaum and Jonathan F. S. Post (San Marino: Huntington Library, 2002), pp. 39-61 (p. 43).

8   *The Oxford Authors: John Clare*, ed. by Eric Robinson and David Powell (Oxford: Oxford University Press, 1984).

9   Landry, p. 44.

10   David Simpson, 'A Speaking Place: The Matter of Genre in "The Lament of Swordy Well"', *Wordsworth Circle*, 34:3 (2003), 131-4 (p. 131).

11   Simpson, p. 131.

12   Simpson, p. 131.

13   Simpson, p. 133.

14   *Green Writing: Romanticism and Ecology* (New York: St. Martin's Press, 2000), p. 86.

15   Scott McEathron, 'Charles Lamb and John Clare: Friends in the Past', *Charles Lamb Bulletin*, 95 (July 1996), 98-109. Simon Kövesi, 'John Clare, Charles Lamb and the *London Magazine*: "Sylvanus et Urban"', *Charles Lamb Bulletin*, 135 (July 2006), 82-93.

16   *A Descriptive Catalogue of the Library of Charles Lamb* (New York: The Dibdin Club, 1897), p. 16.

17   'Mackery End, in Hertfordshire', *Essays of Elia* (London: Chatto and Windus, 1874), p. 101.

18   'Two Races of Men', *Essays of Elia*, p. 40.

19   'A Complaint of the Decay of Beggars', *Essays of Elia*, p. 149.

20   Emma Trehane, '"Emma and Johnny": The Friendship Between Eliza Emmerson and John Clare', *JCSJ*, 24 (2005), 69-77. Clare MacDonald Shaw, 'Some Contemporary Women Poets in Clare's Library', in *The Independent Spirit: John Clare and the Self-Taught Tradition*, ed. by John Goodridge (Helpston: John Clare Society, 1994), pp. 87-122.

'Botanical arangements': John Clare, Parataxis, and Common Sense

Moinak Choudhury

Reminiscing about his youth in his autobiographical notes, John Clare recalls how his friend Tom Porter's 'fondness for flowers', gardening, and reading books about gardening influenced him.[1] Weekend visits to look at Porter's inheritance — a collection including George Sandy's *Travels* (1673) and John Parkinson's *Theatrum Botanicum* (1640) — offered an acquaintance with the printed word amid otherwise 'sparing' opportunities. Porter's persistent interest (emphasized by Clare's use of both 'bought' and 'buys') in gathering all the 'second hand one[s] that treat upon the subject [of gardening]' furthered this familiarity. However, he adds that their interest in foraging extended beyond bargains for herbals and travelogues. Clare's observation that they also 'usd to go out on Sundays to hunt curious wild flowers to plant in the garden such as orchids' implies that his habits of reading about nature grew alongside measures of caring for the transplants. Elsewhere, reflecting on a similar practice in 'Holywell', Clare watches how the village children pluck daisies and 'show the prize their searches found', not in vases but flowerpots.[2] Like his youthful pursuits with Porter, they simultaneously disturb nature and display 'care and skill' in their encounters. Clare asserts that these boyhood feelings have passed him — he no longer feels the delight in unsettling the 'daisy's earliest prime' and robbing 'every primrose-root I met'.[3] And yet, references to transplantation frequently reoccur across his letters and natural history prose writings.

For instance, writing about the 'Pleasure of Spring', Clare satirizes the 'man of taste' removing primroses to put it 'between the leaves for a mark & pledge of spring', and the poet strolling in search of the divine in the commons.[4] But as Margaret Grainger points out, he also had an extensive collection of local, rare, and very rare orchids, adding that it is 'deeply disturbing to us, in a conservation-conscious

Detail from 'History of a Coat', *Glasgow Looking Glass*, 4 (23 July 1825).

era, to think of anyone uprooting plant specimens to replant in his garden'. Clare's collection of orchids included:

> two specimens of the 'locally common' twayblade, two of the 'local' pyramidal, one each of the 'local' fragrant and bee, six of the 'very local' man, one of the 'not every common' butterfly, one of the 'rather rare' bird's-nest, one of the 'very rare, if not extinct' spider, and one of the extremely rare military orchid for which there is no record in Northamptonshire [and] three specimens of the 'Lily Leaved' and one each of the 'Female or Meadow' and 'Male or Wood'.[5]

Grainger limits the 'infinitesimal' consequences of 'Clare's ravages' by comparing it with the more pernicious plough, which Clare describes as the 'destroyer of wild flowers'.[6] And yet, this ecological tension, apparent in Grainger's sequencing of the list from the 'local' to the 'extremely rare', leaves us with a more enduring query: how does Clare's horticultural practice relate to, or alter, his poetics? Given his habits as a collector, preserver, and gardener, I examine how this intention unsettles his role as a mere observer in nature and enables a search for an alternative ecopoetics. In this essay, I build on this notion through what

Clare terms 'botanical arrangements'. Surveying contemporary approaches to an ecocritical Clare, I then read a selection of his early poems alongside Theodor Adorno's critique of Hölderlin's poetics of genius and nature in 'Parataxis'.[7] Finally, I suggest that given Clare's limitations, we can grasp the nuances of his ecopoetics by returning to eighteenth-century common sense philosophy and its emphasis on the subject's dependence on objects (in our case, nature) outside oneself. My intention here is not to dispute current ecocritical traditions but address the issue of Clare's position as a horticulturist *and* an observer of nature.

Clare's paratactic style — short sentences which do not depend on subordinated clauses — has been a critical component of ecocritical approaches to his works.[8] Notably, John Barrell has shown how the photo-miniatures of rural life and ecology — 'the multiplicity of objects in his field of experience' — represent Clare's rooted sense of place.[9] This manifold of impressions is local, but it does not collapse under a single hierarchical view or fall prey to pathetic fallacy coloring nature with manufactured melancholy.[10] Correspondingly, Stephanie Kuduk Weiner points to Clare's central syntactic strategy during the middle period poems, wherein his paratactic juxtaposition of sounds draws on natural history writers such as Gilbert White.[11] Michael Falk discusses his use of parataxis and 'list-like quality' to demonstrate an 'aesthetic of variety'.[12] And more recently, Scott Hess refers to this style to consider Clare's 'biosemiotic poetics', which decenters the human.[13] It is worth noting here that conventional critiques of the paratactical style's function do not necessarily convey an ecocritical position. In *Mimesis*, Auerbach traces its vital function in the development of both Homeric and Augustinian forms of demonstrating realism through, on the one hand, 'externalized, uniformly illuminated phenomena, at a definite time and in a definite place, connected together without lacunae in a perpetual foreground' and, contrarily, the 'impulsive and dramatic, most often in matters concerned with the inner life' respectively.[14] For Auerbach, the external becomes internal, but the impact of the staccato, impressionistic report endures. However, we can attribute its distinct characterization as a mode resisting the categorizing subject's inclination to subjugate the object to Adorno's remarks on Hölderlin's poetry and how its *fortissimo* combats Heidegger's reading of it as a poetic dwelling. In his 1963 speech, 'Parataxis', Adorno sketches this search for a syntactic style to match the contents of his vision for an autonomous subject — a position which refrains from, on the one hand, complying with available universals and, relatedly, dominating what it observes. Can the combination of intention and poetic form contend with such impositions? Adorno finds such a prospect in Hölderlin's late poetry. He asserts:

> the formal principle of parataxis, an anti-principle, is commensurable as a whole with the intelligible content of Hölderlin's late lyric poetry. It delineates the sphere of the *coincidence* of content and form, their specific unity within the substance of the work. In terms of the content, synthesis or identity is equivalent to the domination of nature. While all poetry protests the domination of nature with its own devices, in Hölderlin the protest awakens to self-consciousness [...] Hölderlin takes the side of fallen nature against a dominating Logos.[15]

In seeking a way out of nature's incorporation under the dominance of *logos*, Hölderlin finds himself. For Adorno, this becomes tenable when he beholds the rough edges of the paratactic style and coincident impressions against the command of polished synthesis and hypotaxis. Although scarcely used in philosophy (as Adorno understood through his unwelcome attempts), the poetic form can craft interconnected lines which juxtapose rather than impose. More importantly, the critic's attention to this style offers a counter to the insufficiency of philological and metaphorical readings of Hölderlin's poems such as 'Winkel von Hardt' ['The Shelter at Hardt']. The poem's 'disturbed character', for Adorno, spills over the confines of certainty and idealism.[16] The meeting of authorial intention and poetic form transforms both elements, rendering the sum of coincidences different (if not greater) than its parts. This metamorphosis takes criticism a few steps beyond the search for disinterested rules. At the same time, Adorno clarifies that while the question of intention and form are not adequate individually, the critic cannot cast both asunder — a method utilized in Heidegger's 'unaesthetic' ordering of Hölderlin's poetics. Heidegger, for Adorno, gives the poet a 'metaphysical dignity [...] without considering the agency of form'.[17] His interpretation is not necessarily arbitrary, but it does not acknowledge the 'truth content's aesthetic medium', despite Heidegger's claim to poetics.[18]

Here Adorno gives the example of Heidegger's references to dwelling in Hölderlin's late poetry, as evident in his reading of the lines, '[f]or that which dwells / Near to its origin hardly will leave the place'.[19] Heidegger may extrapolate it to celebrate an unwrinkled origin; however, the *fortissimo* of 'but' in the subsequent line ('But I will make for the Caucasus!') repels its untethered incorporation into any abstract philosophy.[20] Adorno explains that Heidegger's rogue attempts at such consolidation are more apparent when he turns the 'exiled Hölderlin' into a heroic, 'trustworthy German living abroad' and his 'erotic *imago* of the Mediterranean woman... to [the] praise of German women'.[21] The identity of the German fatherland triumph over preoccupations with the Being. Together, they engulf all the particularities of Hölderlin's poetics and his preoccupation with historical finitude and loss-stricken nostalgia.

To extrapolate the resistance to such synthesis, Adorno posits that Hölderlin's form (as 'sedimented content') and paratactic style embody a mode in which 'the familiar becomes the unfamiliar'. Like the sonata, they appear as 'discrete contrasting units within a unity' which 'gently suspends the traditional logic of synthesis'.[22] Hölderlin's striking impressions and its 'artificial disturbances' evade judgment and 'the logical hierarchy of a subordinating syntax'.[23] For Adorno, this manner of thinking rivals the primacy of content, even contradicting Hölderlin's intention in the process. By negating synthesis and juxtaposing different timelines and clauses, he simply observes.

Adorno's reading of Hölderlin attenuates the issue of the interfering subject in nature. But in formulating Hölderlin's antithesis to idealism and logos, he nevertheless runs into the problem of the poet's position and relation to the environment: how does he observe and maintain the contradictions of the particulars without individual (if not a general) synthesis? Hölderlin sides with nature and provides an 'anamnesis of art's protest against rationality', but to what extent can we divest his use of rationalizing and his choice of the poetic medium?[24] Does impression not threaten to organize if not synthesize the object of observation? In attempting to solve this problem, Adorno returns, a bit unconvincingly, to idealism and formulates 'the reconciliation of genius and nature' to negotiate this precarious stance. He emphasizes the natural characteristic of genius — its openness and 'naked and unarmed quality that distinguishes it from the prevailing spirit'.[25] Genius can cancel the cycle of domination over nature, for it is 'not wholly unlike nature'.[26] And like nature, genius reconciles what lies beyond itself without collapsing it under a singular identity. Finally, Adorno collapses the difference altogether, stating, '[g]enius itself is also nature'.[27] This problem of organizing and parataxis in Adorno's reading similarly applies to Clare. Indeed, in 'Helpstone', Clare portrays his tussle as the 'low genius' caught between the impositions of the 'vulgar & the vain'; the former's opinions 'subdue' the possibility of 'rising thoughts'; the latter's envy 'damps each humble view'.[28] But his horticultural practice disturbs an alignment with Adorno's notion of the naked, unassuming genius. The matter of Clare's horticultural poetics (if I may call it so) then requires another approach that can contend with, on the one hand, the problem of domination and, contrarily, Clare's relation with his environment. Instead of a definite paratactic mode, I turn to the ways in which Clare's attenuated parataxis uses distinct impressions organized within a loosely interconnected process.[29] In fact, reminiscing on his poetic career, Clare writes to his son Charles that his particular form involves, as he says, 'botanical arangements':

> I wrote or rather thought Poems made botanical arangements when a little Boy which men read and admired   I loved nature and painted her both in words and colours better then many Poets and Painters[30]

This ecopoetic exhibition reconciles the horticulturist and the poet. It presents a style tethered to its local and historical content. More importantly, the notion of arrangement speaks to Adorno's emphasis on coincidence and juxtaposition of the paratactic style rather than synthesis. Like the early modern cabinet of curiosities, the objects in Clare's poetic commons recreate the possibility of free association lost in the ecological commons.[31] But the organizer's hand remains visible.

Returning to 'Helpstone', we find, for instance, Claire's self-portrait as a poet unwillingly fastened to his location — a place where progress remains interrupted, where 'dawning genius never met the day'.[32] The impossibility of change in universal time and local time at Helpstone restricts both personal evolution and movement. Rest appears inescapable due to the unceasing sense of 'doubtful end' that mars labours, journeys, and fates alike.[33] Placed within nature, the coordinator 'so' sets the reader's expectations for a similar sedate moment in the following stanza: like Helpstone's low genius, the 'little birds in winter' search for 'food & "better life" in vain'.[34] However, the observer now notices how they are surprisingly 'glad to seek the place from whence they went / & put up with distress & be content —'.[35] Instead of perceiving a beginning and end, the em dash (—) marks the cyclicity of nature's labour which continues despite the stifling monotony. More importantly, it signals how this spiraling movement, albeit circumscribed by its radius, generates a shift in perspective: amid the prevailing stasis he now recognizes a sense of home, a 'place from whence they went', fueling their persistence.

This study of time and motion furrows a turn in the observer's attitude. And we note its effects in the following stanza which echoes the initial survey of Helpstone:

> Hail scenes obscure so near & dear to me
> The church the brook the cottage & the tree
> Still shall obscurity reherse the song
> & hum your beauties as I stroll along
> Dear native spot which length of time endears
> The sweet retreat of twenty lingering years[36]

In this occurrence, Clare turns to 'scenes obscure' that are 'so near' and 'dear to me', tethering obscurity and proximity. We expect Clare to present another picture of futility and melancholy. And yet, this paradox turns the distressing landscape into a photo-miniature that Clare carries as he 'stroll[s] along'; its contradictions spring a newfound progression in space and time. Facing the effects of the enclosure movement, Clare does 'mourn' for the loss of the 'vanish'd green', but this shift presents something quite different from the sense of the helpless genius stuck in Helpstone.[37] It is now flux and fear of loss rather than the anxiety of stasis that connects the images:

> How oft I've sighd at alterations made
> To see the woodmans cruel axe employ'd
> A tree beheaded or a bush destroy'd
> Nay e'en a post (old standards) or a stone
> Moss'd o'er by age & branded as her own
> Would in my mind a strong attachment gain
> A fond desire that there they might remain[38]

John Barrell reads these lines as an example of parataxis where 'there is no attempt to connect the landscape with a conventional melancholy of Clare's own'.[39] However, we note that Clare intersects the surrounding landscape with the same erosion that the wandering, unsettled poet faces. More significantly, the object repels the subject's initial categorization and, in turn, occasions 'a strong attachment' and a metacognitive change: the observer fails in his hasty classification, and the obscure, hazy view that we began with gives way to a detailed sketch of a 'long evanish'd scene' mapped with coordinates provided by adverbs of place and time, 'where' and 'so'. The last stanza summarizes this altered perspective wherein, like the birds, '[e]ach hated track so slowly left behind' now provides directions for 'the home which night denies to find'.[40] Rather than a list of disparate descriptions, we find carefully correlated images that reconcile nature's work and the poet's labour.

By arranging the coincidence between nature and thought, Clare inverts the dynamics of political ecology through the attenuated paratactic style. A single moment correlates with another unrelated instance. However, on stepping back, we see a chain of impressions leading to a grander realization. Instead of merely lamenting enclosure or the loss of openness, the stanzas mimic the commons, preserving where they can, showing their epistemological function elsewhere. Fences interrupt free associative thinking, but his verses continue to till the landscape, searching for lasting interrelations. We see this effect of framed sequences (rather than disparate sketches) in the title of the sonnet, 'The Gipsies Evening Blaze'. Here the absence of the noun's possessive form suspends the otherwise subordinated relation between the subject and their belonging. The poem similarly underscores this coincidence between nature and man:

> *Where sudden starts* the quivering blaze behind
> Short shrubby bushes nibbl'd by the sheep
> That alway on these shortsward pastures keep
> *Now* lost *now* shines *now* bending with the wind
> And *now* the swarthy sybil [k]neels reclin'd
> With proggling stick she still renews the blaze
> Forcing bright sparts to twinkle from the flaze[41]

The blaze appears to begin in a pasture without an external agent, reinforced by its location — 'where Boreas has no power'.[42] The rapidly repeating adverb 'now' cleaves a moment into multiple snapshots, supplying a frame-by-frame report locating changes in time, place, and the blaze's elemental character as it leaps from the bush to the pasture as a glimmer in the wind. The fire's dependence on an external agent is only apparent when it needs to be restoked. More significantly, these observations leave a lasting effect on the viewer's 'attentive mind', who will henceforth 'oft exclaim [...] / "Grant me this life, thou spirit of the shades!"'[43] Like a rapidly moving blaze, a singular moment sparks the potential for a grand philosophic realization concerning first, nature's interconnected elements at work, and second, a metacognition that the observer's intellectual labour depends on such coincidences.

At other moments in his early poems, Clare is almost aphoristic in his observation. For instance, in 'Summer Evening' we follow his gaze to see how the sparrows picking up 'the inscet from your grounds' is a distinct sign of how 'providence [...] / Sends nothing here without its use'.[44] And yet, when read as a sequence that begins with the first line of 'The sinken sun is takin leave', we find that the listicle of observations is bound to a common, progressive timeline.[45] Similar markers of time and juxtaposed events occur in 'The Harvest Morning' and 'The Woodman', where the crowing cock and the snow-clad bell set distinct images of rural life into motion like the parts of a grand automaton.[46] Combining the pastoral idyll and a georgic landscape of labour, this sense of watching nature and society at work and how that work fosters cognitive change is more explicitly apparent in how adverbs of time hinge the poem 'Evening' around disparate but interwoven moments.

> Now grey ey'd hazy eve's begun
> To shed her balmy dew—
> Insects no longer fear the sun
> But come in open view
>
> Now buzzing with unwelcome din
> The heedles beetle bangs
> Agen the cowboys dinner tin
> That oer his shoulder hangs[47]

Like the hands of a clock, 'now' indicates both the arrival of a scene and its departure. But more importantly, one sequence of events engenders the next, beginning with the shift from obscurity to clarity, and sound sparks action which 'But buzzes on till batter'd down / For unmeant Injury given'.[48] Instead of silence, we find an exposition which sets into motion an expanding argument nestled between sets of 'now' and 'but', openings and closures, signs of life and rest. Significantly, this series of 'distant objects dimly seen' also cause a strong attachment. Only after observing nature at work does the plough man find his coda as he 'argues to himself': '"Now

I am left the fallow Clods / I'm happy & I'm free'".[49] Although
the paratactic style cleaves the individual moments, the clauses
reconcile around a sequence set in play by dusk's first light and end
with a philosophical realization.

This attention to Clare's attenuated paratactic style still leaves
us with the issue of the subject's place in his environment. Clare
watches both nature and human labour; but given his horticultural
poetics, how can we situate the observer without recourse to the
non-intrusive genius? Instead of seeking an exception, we might
find such a figure in the commons, or more specifically, Clare's
references to common sense, which appear in myriad forms across
his works. He includes them in pithy statements scattered across
his prose — 'pretending perfection in this world is to common
sense a painted Sepulchre' — where it signifies a form of self-
evident knowledge that can slice through the abstract distinctions
between the living and the dead.[50] Elsewhere, he uses it to refer to
the Swing riots stating that 'Common sense would never covet the
property that belongs to another'.[51] In fact, writing to Martha Clare
in 1849-50, Clare also shows his understanding of Tom Paine's
version of common sense and the rights of man. He cites it in
his letters and notes from the Northampton period to frame his
detainment at the asylum as evidence of a resistant individualism
amid governmental overreaches.

> Truth wether it enters the Ring or the Hall of Justice shows a plain
> Man that is not to be scared at shadows or big words full of fury and
> meaning nothing   when done and said with them truth is truth
> and no further and the rights of man — age of reason and common
> sense are sentences full of meaning and the best comment of its
> truth is themselves —[52]

But contrary to the 'full meaning' of common sense and the age
of reason, Clare also underscores the restrictions of collective
knowledge. For instance, he points to how he used to draw on his
family's review of his early work to edit its reach and language: 'I
thought if they coud not understand me my taste shoud be wrong
founded and not agreeable to nature, so I always strove to shun it
for the future and wrote my pieces according to their critisisms'.[53]
He then remarks on his later realization about the limitations of
this critique which left his work 'fit for nothing but mothers old
purposes'. Common sense's utility for a low genius in Helpston
limits spatial and intellectual progress. As P. M. S. Dawson

points out, common sense in Clare 'remains for him universal from which particularly interests depart' while acknowledging the restrictions of this class consciousness that is not necessarily revolutionary for him.[54]

Apart from these connotations, we might see Clare's common sense through another form of knowing and arranging that borrows from nature and notes its capacity to leave strong attachments. This manner of nature-human relations is not unlike the common sense perception outlined in Thomas Reid's *An Inquiry into the Human Mind on the Principles of Common Sense* (1764). Scholars approach Reid's theories of common sense, or direct realism, in the context of the Lockean ideal system – that is, a mode of perception where the mind only takes ideas as its object: '[Idealists think that] we do not really perceive things that are external, but only certain images and pictures of them imprinted upon the mind, which are called impressions and ideas'.[55] Reid rejects the way idealism subjugates the existence of external things into internal images, as purely data, to comprehend perception. Instead, the onus of agency is equally divided: when 'we perceive objects, we act upon them or they upon us *immediately*'.[56] My intention here is not to recount his argument against idealism. Rather, I suggest that a closer look shows that Reid's natural philosophy provides something more nuanced for our reading of Clare's horticultural poetics — a prospect for understanding the unmediated perception characteristic of his paratactic style without disavowing his role in organizing, selecting, and arranging them. In this regard, Reid underscores an end to philosophical squabbles by advocating for common sense, but more importantly, a mind-independent world of objects and relations. Besides an anti-idealist stand, he emphasizes a universe's 'permanent existence' outside the human mind:

> Ideas seem to have something in their nature unfriendly to other existences [...] since men began to reason clearly and distinctly about them, they have [...] undermined the existence of every thing but themselves.[57]

In the grounds of common sense judgment and its awareness of nature's subjugation, we find an alternative to seeing Clare as dwelling, decentering or becoming a genius in nature.[58] Instead, for an active horticulturist like Clare and his poetics of capturing nature at work, we note a similar dependence on the perception of objects outside the self and their subsequent arrangement. Albeit plucked by Clare, they make their strong attachment felt even outside their native place. To be sure, Reid's common sense does not provide a negation of hierarchies between man and nature that we might seek. But neither does Clare. However, when we trace Clare's repeated reference to impressions where distant objects dimly seen turn to juxtapositions of obscurity and clarity, and finally lead to a metacognitive change in the observer, we repeat Reid's notion of direct realism. Hence, in the 'Reccolections after a Ramble', the coincidence of images move through the day; this sequence follows the end of both the brown lark's summer anthem and the prevailing inertia when it 'trembling' drops the corn on the pasture below.[59] Clare carefully arranges each paratactic sequence as it cycles through labour and rest until he professes his love for 'Rurallity' whose 'sweetness yields to none', adding that 'These with nature shall prevail / When epics war harps broke in two'.[60] Like Reid's direct realism, it is precisely the object's resilience against subordination and incorporation into anthems of history and abstraction which occasions its preservation beyond the subject's mediated narration.

NOTES

1   *By Himself*, p. 51.
2   *Early Poems*, II, p. 46, ll. 132-5
3   *Early Poems*, II, p. 46, ll. 142-3.
4   *Natural History*, p. 278.
5   *Natural History*, pp. 295-6.
6   *Natural History*, p. 295.
7   Theodor W. Adorno, 'Parataxis: On Hölderlin's Late Poetry', *Notes to Literature*, ed. by Rolf Tiedemann, trans. by Shierry Weber Nicholsen (New York: Columbia University Press, 2019), pp. 376-412. Henceforth referred to as 'Parataxis'.
8   Such an emphasis on form and Clare's ecopoetic style is, of course, not exhaustive. See, for instance, Timothy Morton, 'John Clare's Dark Ecology', *Studies in Romanticism*, 47.2 (2008), 179-93 (pp. 183; 191); Emma Mason, 'Ecology with religion: kinship in John Clare', *New Essays on John Clare*, ed. by Simon Kövesi and Scott McEathron, (Cambridge: Cambridge University Press, 2015), pp. 97-117 (p. 113); and W. John Coletta, 'Ecological Aesthetics and the Natural History Poetry of John Clare', *JCSJ*, 14 (1995), 29-46.
9   John Barrell, *The Idea of Landscape and the Sense of Place* 1730-1840 (Cambridge: Cambridge University Press, 2015), p. 151.
10 Patrick Bresnihan also adds how Clare's style 'resist metaphor, leaving no margin for expansion beyond the particular act of hearing or seeing things in the moment, the singularity of each concurrence'. See Patrick Bresihan, 'John Clare and the Manifold Commons. *Environmental Humanities*, 3.1 (2013), 71-91. (p. 77).

11   Stephanie Kuduk Weiner, 'Listening with John Clare', *Studies in Romanticism*, 48.3 (2009), 371-90 (p. 380). Weiner, however, adds that unlike White's temporal connection between events, Clare presents a 'coherent music' which interrelating both sound and image (pp. 381-2).

12   Michael Falk, 'The Nightjar's Shriek: Nature's Variety in the Sonnets of John Clare and Charlotte Smith', *JCSJ*, 36 (2017), 31-48 (p. 43).

13   Scott Hess, 'Biosemiosis and Posthumanism in John Clare's Multi-Centered Environments', *Palgrave Advances in John Clare Studies*, ed. by Simon Kövesi and Erin Lafford (London: Palgrave Macmillan, 2020) pp. 199-219 (pp. 200; 205).

14   Erich Auerbach, *Mimesis*, trans. by Willard R. Trask (Princeton: Princeton University Press, 2003), p. 11; p. 71.

15   'Parataxis', pp. 376-412 (p. 403; my emphasis).

16   'Parataxis', p. 378.

17   'Parataxis', p. 380.

18   'Parataxis', p. 381.

19   'Parataxis', p. 383.

20   'May the one who has tested it believe! for the spirit is at home / Not in the beginning, not at source' (qtd. in Adorno, 'Parataxis', p. 383).

21   'Parataxis', p. 384.

22   'Parataxis', pp. 394-5. See also Adorno's notion of 'natural beauty' in *Aesthetic Theory*. The '[q]uasi-rational tendencies of art', for Adorno, diminishes its 'immediate experience'. Theodor W. Adorno, *Aesthetic Theory*, ed. by Gretel Adorno and Rolf Tiedeman, trans, by Robert Hullot-Kentor (Minneapolis, Minn.: University of Minnesota Press, 1997), pp. 65-6.

23   'Parataxis', p. 395.

24   'Parataxis', p. 407.

25   'Parataxis', pp. 408-9. For Adorno's notion of genius and nature, see also *Aesthetic Theory*, p. 171, where Adorno posits the genius as 'the potential enemy of artworks' which also 'becomes the proxy' for what is 'denied to humanity as a whole'.

26   'Parataxis', p. 410.

27   'Parataxis', p. 411.

28   *Early Poems*, I, p. 156, ll. 9-12.

29   See also Brian Reed's assertion that Hart Crane's poetry uses tenuously interconnected clauses or 'attenuated hypotaxis', in *Hart Crane: After his Lights* (Tuscaloosa: University of Alabama Press, 2006), pp. 118-9. I use attenuated parataxis to preserve, as we saw in Auerbach's *Mimesis*, its historical use to depict realism and immediacy.

30   *By Himself*, p. 277.

31   For the early modern cabinet of curiosities see Barbara M. Benedict, *Curiosity: a Cultural History of Early Modern Inquiry* (Chicago: University of Chicago Press), 2001; Marjorie Swann, *Curiosities and Texts the Culture of Collecting in Early Modern England* (Philadelphia: University of Pennsylvania Press), 2001; and Peter Harrison, 'Curiosity, Forbidden Knowledge, and the Reformation of Natural Philosophy in Early Modern England', *Isis*, 92.2 (2001), 265–90.

32   *Early Poems*, I, p. 156, l. 7.

33   *Early Poems*, I, pp. 156-7, l. 14; l. 18; l. 22.

34   *Early Poems*, I, p. 157, ll. 23 and 25.
35   *Early Poems*, I, p. 158, ll. 45-6.
36   *Early Poems*, I, p. 158, ll. 47-51.
37   *Early Poems*, I, p. 159, ll. 73-4.
38   *Early Poems*, I, p. 159, ll. 86-92.
39   Barrell, p. 114.
40   *Early Poems*, I, p. 163, l. 184.
41   *Early Poems*, I, p. 33, ll. 5-11 (my emphasis).
42   *Early Poems*, I, p. 33, l. 4.
43   *Early Poems*, I, p. 33, l. 14.
44   *Early Poems*, I, p. 10, ll. 146, 149, 151.
45   *Early Poems*, I, p. 5, l. 1.
46   *Early Poems*, I, pp. 434-7; *Early Poems*, II, pp. 287-97.
47   *Early Poems*, I, p. 388, ll. 1-8.
48   *Early Poems*, I, p. 388, ll. 15-16.
49   *Early Poems*, I, p. 391, ll. 81-2.
50   *By Himself*, p. 30. For the multiple connotations of common sense in Clare's
      works see P. M. S. Dawson, 'Clare and the ideology of 'common sense', *JCSJ*,
      16 (1997), 71-80.
51   *By Himself*, p. 59.
52   *By Himself*, p. 281.
53   *By Himself*, p. 14.
54   Dawson, pp. 75-6.
55   Thomas Reid, *An Inquiry into the Human Mind on the Principles of Common
      Sense*, ed. by Derek R. Brookes, (Pennsylvania: Pennsylvania State University
      Press), 1997, p. 4. For Locke and Reid, see Ryan Nichols, *Thomas Reid's
      Theory of Perception* (Oxford: Clarendon Press, 2007), pp. 161-84, and James
      van Cleeve 'Reid's Theory of Perception', *The Cambridge Companion to
      Thomas Reid*, ed. by Terence Cuneo and Rene van Woudenberg (Cambridge:
      Cambridge University Press, 2006), pp. 101-4. For a succinct overview of
      direct realism see Christopher A. Shrock, *Thomas Reid and the Problem of
      Secondary Qualities*, (Edinburgh: Edinburgh University Press, 2017), pp. 1-27.
56   Van Cleve, p. 102.
57   Reid, *An Inquiry into the Human Mind*, pp. 33-4.
58   For an overview of ecocritical approaches to the eighteenth century, see
      Christopher Hitt, 'Ecocriticism and the Long Eighteenth Century', *College
      Literature*, 31.3 (2004), 123–47. Erin Drew and John Sitter. 'Ecocriticism and
      Eighteenth-Century English Studies'. *Literature Compass*, 8.5 (2011), 227–39.
      However, they do not consider Reid's place within this ambit.
59   *Early Poems*, II, p. 187, ll. 1-4.
60   *Early Poems*, II, p. 196, ll. 251-6.

Textures of John Clare's Sonnets: A Corpus-Based Structural Comparison between Three Master Sonneteers

Kazutake Kita

John Clare, 'the greatest labouring-class poet England ever gave birth to',[1] could also be counted among the masters of sonnet writing in the early nineteenth-century Britain. Arunodoy Bhattacharyya's pioneering study in the sonnets by English Romantic poets, though not clear about the sources he used, gives the figures of the sonnets written by major poets: the outstanding number of 523 by Wordsworth overwhelms Keats's 67, Coleridge's 48, and less than 20 by Shelley and Byron.[2] Given that these figures serve as a rough sketch of the time, Clare's number of 638 is a remarkable feat.[3] There is therefore ample evidence to support the claim that 'John Clare was a major sonneteer'.[4]

After a revival in late eighteenth-century England, the sonnet as a form had established its position by the beginning of the nineteenth century as 'a staple of English poetry'.[5] As indicated by cautious descriptions in an encyclopedia – wherein a sonnet is 'normally' in iambic pentameter, consisting of fourteen lines 'whose rhyme scheme varies despite the assumption that the sonnet form is fixed'[6] – the sonnet has fostered variation and deviation in different ages and through a variety of poets. Romantic-period poets have long been recognized for the innovations they brought to – and the possibilities they opened for – this traditional form. Clare's sonnets have also been discussed along these lines, and his distinctive, experimental, and idiosyncratic approaches towards the genre have been discussed quite widely by critics.[7]

These discussions, however, have not yet exhausted the topics to be considered, with at least two issues almost untouched. First, despite the fact that the internal construction of the sonnet form can be characterized on the one hand by its rhyme scheme and on the other hand by its metrical structure, discussions have often been preoccupied with the former, while the latter has gone unheeded. Put in other words, the sonnet as a type of 'text' (a word with an etymological relationship with 'textile') has been analyzed from the perspective of its features observed in the vertical direction, while those in the horizontal direction have received much less scholarly attention; the texture of a textile comes from the weave of its warp and woof, and without either of them it is no longer a textile at all.

Further complicating the matter is that since the conventional analysis of sonnets has emphasized the singularity of each piece of work, it has not necessarily been made clear what kind of general inclination or bias the poet might have had in handling this specific form, or what overall tendency might be observed in the poet's sonnets. This is an inevitable corollary of the methodology developed in the humanities, and as such it would be unproductive to find fault with its fundamentals. Nevertheless, as long as Clare's sonnets are illuminated solely in this light, the criteria for their distinctiveness[8] or idiosyncrasy[9] always remain in the hands of those who mention them, leaving open such questions as to whether the distinctiveness or idiosyncrasy is found in Clare's sonnets as a whole, how distinctive or idiosyncratic they are in comparison with the works of other contemporary poets, and how that evaluation can be justified. To bridge this gap, some method other than close reading is required.

One exceptional study in this context is by Michael Falk, in an essay in this journal in 2017. His comparison of Clare's sonnets with those of Charlotte Smith and William Wordsworth, buttressed by statistical data concerning rhyme schemes, rich rhymes, and the use of 'and', takes a significant step towards solving the latter of the two above-mentioned problems. As stressed by Tim Chilcott,[10] and despite words of warning from Sara Guyer,[11] numerical information can offer insight into our understanding of Clare's oeuvre.

The analysis that follows can be regarded as an extension of Falk's work, with the remaining issue of metrical structure kept in view. This essay focuses on three major sonneteers of early nineteenth-century England: John Clare, William Wordsworth, and John Keats. It investigates the texture of their sonnets, with the aim of giving a further statistically-grounded explanation for the acclaimed distinctiveness and idiosyncrasy of Clare's work. The choice of Wordsworth and Keats (whose influence on Clare's sonnets he implicitly or explicitly expresses in sonnet form[12]) resulted partly because they are ranked first and second in Bhattacharyya's estimation of the number of sonnets credited to major Romantic poets, and also because their names are included along with Clare's in the same series of poetry anthologies, which was convenient in the author's sampling process.

To be more specific, the present study has three research tasks to be tackled. The first is to describe the textural characteristics of Clare's, Wordsworth's, and Keats's sonnets in terms of both their rhyme scheme and metrical structure and thus to clarify the position of the three poets' (especially Clare's) works through statistical comparison. Closely related to this is the second task, which is to explore the means of representing textural tendencies of the sonnets by the three poets in as accurate and visually-graspable a manner as possible. This may seem like sowing the wind and reaping the whirlwind: the problem itself has been brought forth by the author's own textile metaphor for describing the sonnet form, and in this sense the task does not necessarily address any pressing academic issue. Nevertheless, if there really is an accessible method for cross-modal translation of sound elements into some visual form, it may soften the resistance towards arcane technical descriptions of poetic forms and contribute to opening poetry studies to a broader audience.

Assuming that these tasks are achieved with satisfactory descriptions of the textures of Clare's sonnets, the third task is to identify the factors that can explain the characteristic features. As far as the present study is concerned, it is virtually impossible to attribute the textural characteristics simply to the factor of the poet's intention; it seems implausible to consider that a specific distribution of rhyme schemes and metrical structures observed in Clare's sonnets is the product of his scrupulous attention to the general proportion of all his works created in his lifetime. Rather, the textures revealed in this study may better be regarded as the traces of the poet's habitual creative practice.

1. Research Method
1.1 Samples and Tools
The main method adopted here is not close reading of individual sonnets but rather distant reading[13] of each poet's sonnets in the aggregate; one of the factors that might determine the success or failure of the study is whether appropriate samples are available for analysis. The matter was not so simple, however: regardless of the accuracy of Bhattacharyya's estimation, it is at least obvious that the sonnets of the two prolific poets vastly outnumber those of Keats, whose literary career was cut short by premature death.

To guarantee a fair comparison between the three poets, it was necessary to prepare three groups of samples, each of which included a comparable number of sonnets with a similar extent of representativeness. In this sense it was a lucky coincidence that the anthologies of all the three poets were included in 'The Major Works' series of Oxford World Classics.[14] When sonnet sequences are also counted in stanza by stanza, the anthologies included 117 sonnets of Clare's, 58 of Wordsworth's, and 48 of Keats's; from these samples the author compiled three mini-electronic corpora for the sonnets by the three poets, with a number (from 01 to 14) attached to each line.

Another factor that makes a big difference to the outcomes of distant reading is whether the researcher has at hand any effective and efficient means to count target features in the samples and give them a statistical meaning. One such tool is *AntConc* (Version 3.4.4), a multi-functional concordancer containing several tools.[15] As will be elaborated, the present study often required the author to make a list of different features found in the corpora and identify how many of the samples were categorized into each type; whether it was a list of rhyme schemes (e.g. Petrarchan, Shakespearean, couplets) or of metrical structures, the process was aided by *AntConc*'s Word List Tool, whose function is exactly dedicated to listing and counting all targeted features in a corpus. Also significant for the purpose of this study was *AntConc*'s Keyword List Tool, which is designed to compare two different corpora, identify the salient words whose frequency is disproportionately higher in either of them, and calculate the extent of the saliency ('Keyness'); this function enabled the author to observe specific differences between the sonnets by three poets in terms of the vocabulary used in them.

One reservation about the keyword analysis of this kind, however, should be mentioned: since the keyword analysis is usually based on the assumption that the two corpora being compared are different in any way, it tends to place too much emphasis on differences while not paying sufficient attention to similarities,[16] still less to the extent to which they are similar to each other. To compensate for this weakness, the author used *Microsoft Excel* to calculate the similarity of the data gained from the corpora. Among several possible methods of computation, the author adopted cosine similarity[17] for comparing two data with many variables, and correlation coefficient[18] when the comparison is concerned with only two variables.

1.2 Step 1: Identifying Rhyme Schemes

With all these samples and tools oriented towards distant reading, however, the first step for this study heavily depended on the manual input of the author: the author analyzed the rhyme schemes found in the three poets' sonnets simply by reading each individual work. There are both negative and positive reasons: on the negative side, the criteria for identifying rhyming pairs often involve some irregularities (e.g. concerning such pairs as come/home and rag/drags), and it is difficult to automate the entire procedure; on the positive side, the total number of sonnet samples, 223, is manageable for one human analyzer. After all, the author (1) described the rhyme schemes observed in the samples as 14-letter strings (e.g. *abbaabbacdecde*) and created for each poet a file only containing the strings, (2) processed the files with *AntConc*'s Word List Tool to list the types of rhyme scheme and their frequency, (3) calculated the cosine similarities between the three poets, and (4) identified the typical or representative rhyme scheme for each poet's sonnets. The results are shown later in Table 1.

1.3 Step 2: Identifying Metrical Structures

The second step of analyzing metrical structures was much more time-consuming, even with the aid of the tools for computation. The biggest challenge came from the need to create a mini-pronunciation dictionary specifically dedicated to this study, one containing the information of stressed/unstressed syllables for each word (e.g. 'w[eak]' for 'the', 's[trong]' for 'bird', 'sw' for 'sonnet', 'swsw' for 'solitary'). On the one hand, it would serve as a uniform criterion for automated judgment of pronunciation and

'Lady with the Rooks', Edward Calvert, 1829, wood engraving.
Metropolitan Museum of Art, New York.

thus help avoid undesirable irregularities. On the other hand, in the sonnet corpora there were many words which were supposed to be pronounced differently in different contexts (e.g. 'where' both as a stressed interrogative adverb and an unstressed relative adverb), and this syntactic judgment still required the author's input. Furthermore, even without such a complication, the author had to check each word's pronunciation prescribed in dictionaries (he consulted *Kenkyūsha's New English-Japanese Dictionary (6th edn)*, *Kenkyūsha's English-Japanese Dictionary For The General Reader (3rd edn)*, and *Oxford English Dictionary Second Edition on CD-ROM (v. 4.0.0.3)* in this order of priority), the process of which was simply a manual job.

Thus the author: (1) processed the whole sonnet corpora with *AntConc's* Word List Tool to list all the vocabulary used in the three poets' sonnets; (2) created a mini-pronunciation dictionary including 5,895 words; (3) processed the sonnet corpora and the pronunciation list with *Microsoft Excel* to automatically convert all the sonnet lines in the former to letter strings consisting only of s's, w's, and line numbers from 01 to 14 (e.g. *wswswswsws03*) and created for each poet a file only containing the strings; (4) processed the files with *AntConc's* Word List Tool to list the types of metrical structures and their frequency; (5) calculated the cosine similarities between the three poets; and, finally, (6) identified the typical or representative metrical structure for each poet's sonnets. The results are shown in Table 2.

1.4 Step 3: Visualizing Textures

The files of metrical structures produced in the second step could be used for another purpose: since each letter string in the files had its line number, it was now possible to examine whether there was any difference between line positions concerning metrical structures. If each of the three poets has a distinctive tendency to use a specific type of metrical structure at each line position of their sonnets, their different preferences should directly lead to different sonnet textures; when this information is woven with the previously acquired information about the distribution of rhyme schemes, everything is ready to visualize the textures of Clare's, Wordsworth's, and Keats's sonnets.

The procedure of visualization is again time-consuming: the author (1) created a chessboard-like grid in which each square box represented one syllable position in a sonnet; (2) counted the syllables stressed at each position; (3) calculated the probability of stressed syllables being placed at each position; (4) coloured each box according to probability (the higher the likelihood, the darker the box); and (5) identified the typical or representative texture for each poet's sonnet. The results are shown below in Table 3.

1.5 Step 4: Identifying Factors Explaining the Different Textures
After the three steps intended for describing the textures of the three poets' sonnets, the remaining task for the author was to give a tentative explanation, most desirably for all of them, but at least for Clare's. Since the author had the above-mentioned tools suitable for distant reading, he chose to use them in a heuristic manner to obtain some clues. More specifically, the author (1) processed the sonnet corpora with *AntConc*'s Keyword List Tool to identify the keywords of each poet's sonnets in comparison with the others' and (2) further examined whether the distribution and use of these keywords could have any reasonable connection with the characteristic textures. Although it was difficult to find anything remarkable in the keywords of Wordsworth's and Keats's sonnets, Clare's keywords showed some characteristics deserving further investigation, whose results are shown later in Tables 4, 5, and 6.

Rhyme Scheme	Wordsworth		Keats		Clare			Similarity
	Count	%	Count	%	Count	%		
aabbccddeeffgg	0	0	0	0	29	24.79	**Wordsworth & Keats**	0.48
abbaabbacdcdcd	8	13.79	16	33.33	0	0	**Wordsworth & Clare**	0
ababcdcdefefgg	0	0	13	27.08	6	5.13	**Keats & Clare**	0.12
abbaabbacdecde	4	6.90	5	10.42	0	0		
abbaaccadedede	8	13.79	0	0	0	0		
abbaabbacddcdc	5	8.62	0	0	0	0		
abbaabbacdedec	2	3.45	3	6.25	0	0		
ababcdcdeefgfg	0	0	0	0	3	2.56		
abbaabbacdcede	2	3.45	1	2.08	0	0		
abbaabbacdceed	3	5.17	0	0	0	0		
abbaabbacddece	3	5.17	0	0	0	0		
abbaabbacdeecd	3	5.17	0	0	0	0		
Others (96 types)	20	34.48	10	20.83	79	67.52		

Table 1. Preferred rhyme schemes of the three poets and their cosine similarities

Metrical Structure	Wordsworth		Keats		Clare			Similarity
	Count	%	Count	%	Count	%		
wswswswsws	63	7.76	52	7.74	388	23.68	Wordsworth & Keats	0.90
wswswwwsws	38	4.68	37	5.51	113	6.90	Wordsworth & Clare	0.83
wswswswwws	46	5.67	21	3.13	87	5.31	Keats & Clare	0.82
swwswswsws	27	3.33	28	4.17	62	3.79		
wswwwswsws	32	3.94	17	2.53	42	2.56		
sswswswsws	17	2.03	11	1.64	60	3.66		
wwwswswsws	22	2.71	18	2.68	41	2.50		
wsssswsws	6	0.74	4	0.69	49	2.99		
wswssswsws	7	0.86	5	0.74	39	2.38		
swwswwwsws	13	1.69	15	2.23	19	1.16		
wwsswswsws	9	1.11	14	2.08	25	1.53		
swwswswwws	11	1.35	19	2.83	14	0.85		
Others (485 types)	512	64.16	431	64.14	699	42.67		

Table 2. Preferred metrical structures of the three poets and their cosine similarities

2. Results

2.1 Rhyme Schemes of the Three Poets' Sonnets

Table 1 shows the overall distribution of rhyme schemes observed in the three poets' sonnet samples, and the cosine similarities between them. The latter figures are striking: the similarity value between Wordsworth and Keats is neither high nor low enough for any decisive judgment, whereas the one between Clare and Keats is as low as 0.12 and, most impressively, the comparison between Clare and Wordsworth records a rare figure of zero. This means that, although as many as 108 types of rhyme scheme were observed in the three poets' 223 sonnets, none of them were shared between the two prolific sonneteers. While it has been pointed out that Clare relished reading Wordsworth's and Keats's sonnets,[19] there is not a single example in which Clare followed the rhyme scheme most preferred by the two great contemporaries, *abbaabbacdcdcd*, consisting of an octave (or two quatrains) and a sestet. Instead, what distinguishes Clare from the other two is his frequent adoption of seven consecutive couplets (*aabbccddeeffgg*), as is pointed out in Falk's study.[20] As far as rhyme schemes are concerned, Clare is definitely idiosyncratic.

2.2 Metrical Structures of the Three Poets' Sonnets

Table 2 shows the overall distribution of metrical structures observed in the three poets' sonnet samples, and the cosine similarities between them. In comparison with the case of rhyme schemes, the figures do not come as a big surprise; as described in the encyclopedia, the lines in the samples are 'normally' constructed in iambic pentameter, although the extent of that normality seems to be moderate. Nevertheless, it is not to be overlooked that the cosine similarity values between Clare and the other two poets (0.83 and 0.82) are slightly lower than the one between Wordsworth and Keats (0.90); while it is true that all the three poets share the most preferred metrical structure of *wswswswsws*, the percentage for Clare is three times higher than that for Wordsworth or Keats, which means that one in four lines of Clare's sonnets faithfully adhere to the basic metrical rule of the sonnet. This finding supports Lessa's argument about Clare as 'a maker of poems' who could skillfully handle 'the aesthetic demands of a rather rigorously defined form'.[21]

2.3 Textures of the Three Poets' Sonnets

Table 3 shows visualized textures of the three poets' sonnets, based on the data concerning their preference for rhyme schemes and metrical structures. The latter characteristics were translated into different color densities of square boxes according to the probability of syllables being stressed in each position. The former characteristics were regarded as different grouping methods of sonnet lines: for Wordsworth and Keats, the most representative is the Petrarchan structure, whose division of two quatrains and a sestet was represented by putting a thick white line between the units; for Clare, his distinctive choice of seven couplets was represented by thick white lines placed at regular intervals.

Visualized in this manner, the difference between Wordsworth and Keats is very subtle: the Keatsian texture is characterized by the high probability of stress at the fourth and tenth syllables in each line, which suggests the poet's unique mid-line cadence; the Wordsworthian texture may, paradoxically, be distinguished by its lack of modulation or undulation, allowing no easy structural interpretation. By contrast, the visual image of the Clarean texture has a conspicuous, check-like pattern with almost mechanical regularity, which even seems to lend credibility to the anecdote of Clare composing his poetry to the rhythm of his mother's spinning wheel;[22] also notable is the tendency of the sixth syllable, which is less likely to be stressed than the second, fourth, eighth, and tenth syllables, possibly indicating Clare's inclination towards structural symmetry inside his sonnets. If all these observations are correct, it can be argued that, at least in formal terms, the idiosyncrasy of Clare's sonnets is not the outcome of his deviating from the norm; rather, his works are too normal to be considered normal.

Visualized Texture

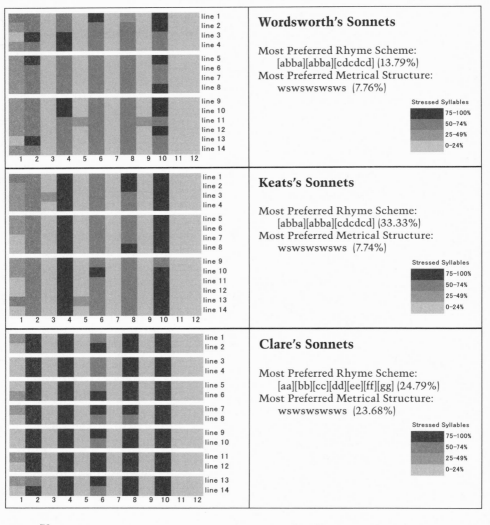

Wordsworth's Sonnets

Most Preferred Rhyme Scheme:
[abba][abba][cdcdcd] (13.79%)
Most Preferred Metrical Structure:
wswswswsws (7.76%)

Stressed Syllables
75–100%
50–74%
25–49%
0–24%

Keats's Sonnets

Most Preferred Rhyme Scheme:
[abba][abba][cdcdcd] (33.33%)
Most Preferred Metrical Structure:
wswswswsws (7.74%)

Stressed Syllables
75–100%
50–74%
25–49%
0–24%

Clare's Sonnets

Most Preferred Rhyme Scheme:
[aa][bb][cc][dd][ee][ff][gg] (24.79%)
Most Preferred Metrical Structure:
wswswswsws (23.68%)

Stressed Syllables
75–100%
50–74%
25–49%
0–24%

Rank	Keywords in Clare's Sonnets (against Wordsworth's)			Keywords in Clare's Sonnets (against Keats's)		
	Keywords	Count	Keyness	Keywords	Count	Keyness
1	the	1092	98.58	and	843	68.64
2	and	843	55.85	the	1092	66.19
3	nest	48	37.75	nest	48	32.09
4	they	95	28.77	they	95	30.11
5	bye	36	28.31	bye	36	24.06
6	oer	33	25.95	up	44	22.34
7	tree	31	24.38	tree	31	20.72

Table 4. Keywords in Clare's sonnets in comparison with Wordsworth's and Keats's

2.4 Factors Explaining the Clarean Texture

In expectation of some explanation for the distinctive texture of Clare's sonnets, the author turned to their keywords. The results shown in Table 4 are just as has often been pointed out by Clare scholars:[23] Clare uses 'and' and 'the' with notably high frequency. The problem here is whether and how this salient use of the two specific words may be linked to the Clarean texture. By intuition, the connection sounds syntactically logical and plausible: 'and' and 'the' (both unstressed) are usually placed next to content words (usually stressed), which would mean that an increased use of 'and' and 'the' leads to an increase of phrases pronounced with alternating rhythm.

To test this hypothesis, the author: (1) counted the frequency of 'and' and 'the' used at each syllable position in Clare's sonnets; (2) visualized the distribution of these two words again on a chessboard-like grid (the higher the frequency, the brighter the box, suggesting that the syllable position is less likely to be stressed); and (3) calculated the correlation coefficient between the probability of each syllable position not being occupied by 'and' or 'the' and that of the same position being stressed. The results are shown in Table 5.

Judging from the correlation coefficients in the table, the infrequency of 'and' alone does not necessarily constitute a strong factor explaining the likelihood of the syllable position being stressed. However, it can safely be said that, at least in Clare's sonnets, the syllable positions without 'and' or 'the' are very likely to be stressed; in other words, the presence/absence of stress at each syllable position in Clare's sonnets is highly predictable from that of 'and' or 'the'. This finding indicates that Clare's distinctive use of these two usually unstressed words is likely to deserve more detailed analysis, and it is here that the method of close reading comes back into the limelight.

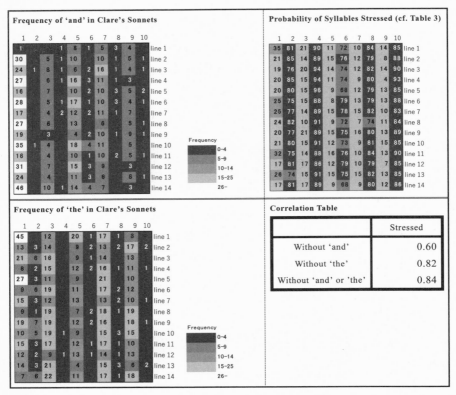

Table 5. Distribution of 'and' and 'the' in Clare's sonnets and its correlation with the probability of syllables being stressed

3. Reading Examples of Clare's Sonnets

Among the samples in the mini corpus, the following could be counted as a good example to show how the Clarean uses of 'and' and 'the' tend to work in his sonnets:

> The sheep get up and make their many tracks
> And bear a load of snow upon their backs
> And gnaw the frozen turnip to the ground
> With sharp quick bite and then go noising round
> The boy that pecks the turnips all the day
> And knocks his hands to keep the cold away
> And laps his legs in straw to keep them warm
> And hides behind the hedges from the storm
> The sheep as tame as dogs go where he goes

And try to shake their fleeces from the snows
Then leave their frozen meal and wander round
The stubble stack that stands beside the ground
And lye all night and face the drizzling storm
And shun the hovel where they might be warm[24]

This 124-word sonnet, titled 'Sheep in Winter' by the editors of the anthology, includes 12 'and's and 15 'the's, which account for more than one in five of the total words in this 14-line poem; furthermore, all of these 27 unstressed words are placed at the odd-numbered syllable positions, thus contributing to the orderly alternating pattern of the Clarean texture.

The distinct dominance of these two words is all the more significant because they seem to be placed at pivotal points and given specific functions in constructing this small piece. First of all, as regards the use of 'the', it is to be noted that this sonnet coheres with the most obvious tendency presented in Table 5: Clare's use of 'the' is the most frequent at the first syllable of the first and fifth lines. In the present example, the role played by 'the' at these two positions cannot be overstated, for they introduce the only two main actors of this sonnet, 'the sheep' and 'the boy'. This fact about 'the' calls attention to another fact, regarding the use of the other unstressed keyword: all the 12 'and's in this sonnet connect verbs, each of which describes the action either of the sheep or the boy. The combined effects of all these could be likened to a short film consisting of a couple of scenes; each 'the' cues a new focal point, and once the focused actor starts to move, then each 'and' changes frames. Collateral evidence from numerical data suggests that this type of plot development in sonnets might be one of Clare's favorite choices: as shown in Table 6, 'and's in Clare's sonnets, usually placed at the first, fifth, or seventh syllable positions, are most often used to connect verbs, and the largest number of this type is observed at the first syllable position of the even-numbered lines. If Clare's sonnets, just as in 'Sheep in Winter', tend to introduce new focal points at the beginning of the odd-numbered lines, then these 'and's of the even-numbered lines are likely to describe the action of the focused actors.

This 'focal-point-and-frame-change' hypothesis about Clare's use of 'the' and 'and' in his sonnets could be verified in two different ways. First, according to the hypothesis, if a focused actor requires more changes of frames, they are likely to be reflected in

Types / Lines	The 1st Syllable		The 5th Syllable		The 7th Syllable		All	
	Odd-num-bered	Even-num-bered	Odd-num-bered	Even-num-bered	Odd-num-bered	Even-num-bered	Odd-num-bered	Even-num-bered
Clause & Clause	50	68	5	10	6	4	69	86
Verb & Verb	45	137	32	66	30	40	135	278
Noun & Noun	17	14	14	21	18	11	81	83
Adjective & Adjective	3	3	8	5	11	6	41	31
Adverb & Adverb	2	2	1	0	3	3	25	10
Others	0	0	1	1	0	0	2	2
Total	117	224	61	103	68	64	353	490

Table 6. Different uses of 'and' and their distribution in Clare's sonnets

the increased number of 'and's. Interesting in this context is the following example, which constitutes the first part of a three-stanza sonnet sequence titled 'Turkeys' by the editors:

> The turkeys wade the close to catch the bees
> In the old border full of maple trees
> And often lay away and breed and come
> And bring a brood of chelping chickens home
> The turkey gobbles loud and drops his rag
> And struts and sprunts his tail and drags
> His wing on ground and makes a huzzing noise
> Nauntles at passer bye and drives the boys
> And bounces up and flyes at passer bye
> The old dogs snaps and grins nor ventures nigh
> He gobbles loud and drives the boys from play
> They throw their sticks and kick away
> And turn agen the stone comes huzzing bye
> He drops his quiet tail and forced to flye [...][25]

This sonnet contains as many as 17 'and's, all of which are again used to connect verbs. The biggest difference from the first example lies in the density of 'and's in specific lines: the turkey focused here 'gobbles loud and drops his rag / And struts and sprunts his tail and drags / His wing on ground and makes a huzzing noise'. A possible interpretation of this distinctive frequency of 'and's may be that, while Clare adopted the same type of plot development in both the first and second examples, the different characteristics of the focused objects (slow sheep and restless turkeys) required different numbers of frames for description.

This interpretation can be extended in a negative direction: if a focused actor requires less changes of frames, they are likely to be reflected in the decreased number of 'and's. A symbolic example here is the following one, which constitutes the first part of a two-stanza sonnet sequence titled 'The Woodlarks Nest' by the editors:

> The woodlark rises from the coppice tree
> Time after time untired she upward springs
> Silent while up then coming down she sings
> A pleasant song of varied melody
> Repeated often till some sudden check
> The sweet toned impulse of her rapture stops
> Then stays her trembling wings and down she drops
> Like to a stone amid the crowding kecks
> Where underneath some hazels mossy root
> Is hid her little low and humble nest
> Upon the ground larks love such places best
> And hers doth well her quiet station suit
> As safe as secresy her six eggs lie
> Mottled with dusky spots unseen by passers bye[26]

As widely recognized, Clare's strong interest in birds provoked a series of nest poems. While this sonnet begins with the introduction of its main character, 'the woodlark', its actions are not traced by 'and's; this piece contains only three 'and's, none of which connect verbs (two for clauses and one for adjectives). Or, in the first place, the woodlark may not be the protagonist, but rather plays a subsidiary role to set the stage for the main focus of the nest, which, by definition, will not move. Thus this sonnet ironically supports the above-mentioned hypothesis with the lack of 'and's: it has only a couple of 'and's, exactly because there is little need for frame changes.

One problem posed here, however, is that, despite the infrequency of 'the' and 'and', this third example still keeps the distinctively orderly rhythm, suggesting that the two unstressed words alone are not enough for explaining the texture of Clare's sonnets. One potential alternative explanation may be that the nest sonnet uses more plurisyllabic words (30, while the first and second ones have 16 and 18 respectively), each of which has a built-in alternating rhythm. Although there is not sufficient space here to discuss this issue, it is at least true that its verification will need more data, hopefully gained from several different perspectives, including both distant reading and close reading methods. The author strongly believes that, when these threads of data are woven together, the Clarean texture will reveal further idiosyncratic characteristics, not yet recognized but surely there.

NOTES

* The origin of this paper is a poster presentation 'Textures of John Clare's Sonnets: A Corpus-Based Structural Comparison between Three Master Sonneteers' presented by the author at the 'Corpora and Discourse International Conference 2020', University of Sussex, June 2020. Much of its content was published in Japanese in *Studies in Liberal Arts and Sciences*, 46 (2021); the present English version includes further revisions and updates.

1   *Biography*, p. 545.
2   Arunodoy Bhattacharyya, *The Sonnet and the Major English Romantic Poets* (Calcutta: Firma KLM, 1976), pp. 1-2.
3   Michael Falk, 'The Nightjar's Shriek: Nature's Variety in the Sonnets of John Clare and Charlotte Smith', *JCSJ*, 36 (2017), 33.
4   Sara Lodge, 'Contested bound: John Clare, John Keats, and the Sonnet', *Studies in Romanticism*, 51 (2012), 533.
5   *A Century of Sonnets*, ed. by Paula R. Feldman and Daniel Robinson (Oxford: Oxford University Press, 2002), p. 3.
6   T. V. F. Brogan, L. J. Zillman, C. Scott, and J. Lewin, 'Sonnet', in *The Princeton Encyclopedia of Poetry and Poetics*, 4th edn, ed. by Ronald Greene, Stephen Cushman, Clare Cavanagh, Jahan Ramazani, Paul Rouzer, Harris Feinsod, David Marno, and Alexandra Slessarev (Princeton: Princeton University Press, 2012), p. 1318.
7   Richard Lessa, 'John Clare's Voice, and Two Sonnets', *JCSJ*, 3 (1984), 26-45; Richard L. Gillin, 'Minute Particulars and Imaginative Forms', *JCSJ*, 5 (1986), 22-9; Andrew Hodgson, 'Form and Feeling in John Clare's Sonnets', *JCSJ*, 31 (2012), 51-66; Stephanie Kuduk Weiner, *Clare's Lyric: John Clare and Three Modern Poets* (Oxford: Oxford University Press, 2014).
8   Lessa, p. 26.
9   Gillin, p. 2; Hodgson, p. 53; Weiner, p. 50.
10 Tim Chilcott, 'John Clare's Language', *JCSJ*, 35 (2016), 5-21.

11 Sara Guyer, *Reading with John Clare* (New York: Fordham University Press, 2015), p. 9. To her question asking whether quantitative approaches can 'help us to track Clare's experience of homelessness and the perspective that this experience offers to our own', the author would hesitantly say 'yes'; being an admirer of Clare's works in spite of his identity as a non-native speaker of English and a non-native of England, any source of information that would bring him close to Clare's real image has been helpful, whether it may be gained through a byway, a side road, or a secret path.

12 Adam White, *John Clare's Romanticism* (London: Palgrave Macmillan, 2017), Ch. 2.

13 Franco Moretti, *Distant Reading* (London: Verso, 2013).

14 John Clare, *Major Works (Oxford World's Classics)* (Oxford: Oxford University Press, 2008); William Wordsworth, *Major Works (Oxford World's Classics)* (Oxford: Oxford University Press, 2008); John Keats, *Major Works (Oxford World's Classics)* (Oxford: Oxford University Press, 2008).

15 Available from <https://www.laurenceanthony.net/software.html> [accessed 31 May 2022].

16 Charlotte Taylor, 'Similarity', in *Corpus Approaches to Discourse: A Critical Review*, ed. by Charlotte Taylor and Anna Marchi (London: Routledge, 2018), pp. 19-37.

17 See Andrew Piper, *Enumerations: Data and Literary Study* (Chicago: The University of Chicago Press, 2018). Cosine similarity is a measure of similarity used in vector space model. Widely adopted in text mining, this model views text documents as bags containing different elements (most usually words) with different frequency, represents the proportion of this frequency as a multi-dimensional vector, and thus calculates similarity between documents as the cosine of the angle of vector arrows (within the range of 0 to 1; the bigger the values are, the more similar the documents). For instance, given three different texts A, B, and C, and if they contain three different pronouns (e.g. 'we,' 'you,' and 'they') with the proportion of 5:3:1, 4:4:1, and 1:2:6 respectively, the cosine value obtained by the comparison between texts A and B is 0.971, while that of texts A and C is 0.449, suggesting the former pair is more similar than the latter.

18 Correlation coefficient is a measure of the extent to which one series of changes in value coordinates with another, thus representing the similarity of the changes within the range of 0 to 1 (or -1 to 0, when the coordinating changes are in the negative direction). If one variable is perfectly in proportion to the other, their correlation coefficient is 1; the lower/higher the correlation coefficient is, the weaker/stronger the two variables are connected.

19 White, Ch. 2.

20 Falk, pp. 39-42.

21 Lessa, p. 26.

22 *Letters*, p. 65.

23 Tim Chilcott, 'An Article on Articles', *JCSJ*, 9 (1990), 31-43; Chilcott, 'John Clare's Language'; Weiner, pp. 34-5; Simon Kövesi, 'Beyond the Language Wars: Towards a Green Edition of John Clare', *JCSJ*, 26, (2007), 61-75; Falk, pp. 41-3.

24 Clare, *Major Works*, p. 263; *Middle Period*, V, p. 252.

25 Clare, *Major Works*, p. 273; *Middle Period*, V, p. 368.

26 Clare, *Major Works*, p. 235; *Middle Period*, IV, pp. 321-2.

The John Clare Society's Annual Festival

Helpston, Saturday 16 July 2022

10.00 a.m. to 7.00 p.m.

A FREE event with the society's AGM, talks, music, tour, bookstalls, poetry readings, refreshments

Come and celebrate the life, work and world of John Clare

For further details contact Sue Holgate
email: smholgate@outlook.com
website: johnclaresociety.wordpress.com

'A Fair – A Group of Gypsies – Men and Women in Rustic Clothes in Front of Two Makeshift Tents', etched by Thomas Rowlandson after Francis Wheatley, 1786. Metropolitan Museum of Art, New York.

John Clare and *The Anniversary*

Robert Heyes

The literary annuals of the 1820s and 1830s are often described as a literary phenomenon, and their success was indeed phenomenal. It was made even more remarkable by the fact that they came to prominence at a time when there was a bank crash and general economic hardship, which affected all parts of the book trade severely. There were bankruptcies among publishers, printers, booksellers and papermakers; Clare's own publishers, Taylor and Hessey, having endured some difficult years, decided that the time had come to end their partnership and go their separate ways. Viewed against this background the rise of the literary annuals was indeed remarkable.[1]

The annuals began with the publication by Rudolf Ackermann of the *Forget-Me-Not* in 1823. It was joined the following year by *Friendship's Offering*, and by 1830 there were around twenty annuals appearing every year. These were small books, typically about six by four inches, or a little smaller. They usually had upwards of three hundred pages, and contained a mixture of poetry and prose, together with about a dozen steel engravings.

There were those in the literary world, at the time and subsequently, who were dismissive of the annuals and their contents. It is only in recent decades that a re-evaluation has taken place, and the literary annuals have come to be seen as worthwhile publications. This has been reflected in the market for these books. Where once they were plentiful and cheap on the secondhand market, they have now become much rarer and much more expensive.

The first work on the annuals was a bibliography of English and American publications, Frederick Faxon's *Literary Annuals and Gift Books*; this was published in 1912 and reprinted with supplementary essays in 1973.[2] The first attempt at classifying the contents of the annuals was made by the Worcester bookseller, Andrew Boyle, in the 1930s. The difficult economic climate of the

'The Bell Inn', George Morland, late 1780s, oil on canvas.
Metropolitan Museum of Art, New York.

times, and the Second World War, prevented publication, and it was
not until 1966 that Boyle's executors published *An Index to the
Annuals*.[3] This lists the authors who contributed to the annuals,
their contributions and which annuals they appear in; a second
volume listing the artists whose work appeared in the annuals was
to have followed, but sadly was never published. Both Faxon's and
Boyle's works remain of value, but both have their inaccuracies
and limitations. A more recent listing is to be found in a doctoral
thesis by Harry Hootman;[4] this discusses various aspects of the
annuals, and also lists the authors, the artists and the engravers who
contributed to them. The most recent, and most valuable, book on
the subject is Katherine D. Harris's *Forget me not: the rise of the
British literary annual, 1823-1835*, reviewed here in 2017.[5]

The contribution of John Clare to the literary annuals has been
little studied, and much of what has been written on the subject
is inaccurate. Some idea of what might be achieved is given by
the treatment of the works of Clare's contemporary, James Hogg.
Volume 17 of the projected 39 volumes of the Stirling/South
Carolina Research Edition of the Collected Works of James Hogg

is devoted to Hogg's contributions to annuals and gift-books.[6] This begins with a historical survey of the annuals, and in particular of Hogg's involvement with them. All of Hogg's contributions are reprinted, and there are lengthy textual and explanatory notes. The whole makes a substantial volume, of nearly five hundred pages. If one searched for anything similar concerning Clare's contributions, one would search in vain; the sum total of the archival research on Clare's poems in the annuals would be a lot nearer to five than five hundred pages.

This is a matter for particular regret because it could be argued that the thirty-nine poems[7] which Clare contributed to the literary annuals were the most important poems he wrote. The four books which Clare published in his lifetime sold well, very well by the standards of the time, but the sales of the more successful annuals were of an order of magnitude greater. The most successful annuals had sales of more than ten thousand copies. Whatever the reservations of some literary people, these were very successful books. They combined the work of the finest writers of the day with the work of the best artists, engraved by the most illustrious engravers. Great attention was paid to the appearance of the annuals, with attractive and often striking bindings being used.[8] They were relatively expensive books and as gift books with, often, an inscription by the donor, they became family heirlooms, being treasured down the generations. Even when a book found its way onto the secondhand market, it was often used for its original purpose years after publication; thus my copy of *The Gem* for 1830 has a presentation inscription dated 1847. David Stewart records that: "The copy of *Friendship's Offering* for 1828 in the National Library of Scotland is inscribed to Mrs Pickersgill, 'the gift of her Sister Mary Hartley, Sep 26th 1838', then again to Susan Nicholson, 'A Birthday Gift from Mother August 19th 1884', and then to H. H. King, 'A Birthday Gift from Mother, March 5, 1937'."[9] These were, then, books which were kept and read throughout the Victorian era and beyond. The Clare poems found in the annuals were the poems of his which were most likely to be read; for nearly a century, indeed, they were the only poems by John Clare which might be encountered by the average reader.

In this brief article I want to concentrate on just one of these poems. It is often said that Clare wrote *for* the literary annuals, but I have no evidence of this. Of course, absence of evidence is not evidence of absence, but in many years of studying Clare's manuscripts and correspondence I have not found any evidence of him doing this. By the time the literary annuals were getting underway, in the mid-1820s, Clare was in his early thirties and, in spite of having published two books, the second of them a two-volume work, as well as poems in the *London Magazine*, he had accumulated a large stock of unpublished verse in manuscript. My impression is that when he received a request for a contribution, from the editor of one of the annuals, he simply sent something from his unpublished manuscript poetry which he thought would be suitable.

I have said 'simply', but in fact there was nothing simple about it. This was, in fact, a very difficult market for the potential contributor to read. The decision as to what to print rested with the editor, and every editor had different requirements. This was partly a matter of personal taste, but it was also a matter of the editor interpreting the wishes of the proprietors of the annual. Each annual rapidly acquired its own character, with some being of a religious bent, others eschewing all such matters, some being light-hearted in tone, others publishing more serious matter, and so on. Thus when, in 1829, he received an invitation to contribute to a new annual, edited by the Revd Thomas Dale, himself a prolific contributor to the annuals, Clare sent what he thought would be an appropriate poem. He received the following reply on 5 November 1829:

Sir,
    I shall feel obliged if you will inform me how I can forward to you £3.3. which Mr Dale & I hope you will do us the favour to accept for your poem, which unfortunately we could not use this year.
    The reason of our not inserting it was partly the great quantity of materials we had, partly the length of your poem, & partly the nature of some of the religious sentiments expressed in it, which my friend, Mr D. thought, I believe, hardly <u>orthodox</u> enough. He intends with your permission, making the necessary curtailments & alterations in it, so as to insert it next year; or should you prefer it, we shall be happy to receive <u>in its stead</u> any other composition of yours which you may think better calculated for our volume.
    I remain, Sir,
    Yours, in haste,
    L. T. Ventouillac[10]

There was to be no 'next year', however, and although Dale went on to edit another short-lived annual, Clare did not contribute. It is worth noting that, although his poem was not used, Clare was paid for it. On the whole the editors of the annuals, probably aware that Clare was not a wealthy man, treated him with great generosity.

Clare had lost the two Stamford friends who might have been of most help in coming to terms with this new literary form. In 1822 Edward Drury had left his bookshop in Stamford and returned to Lincoln to help run the family business, and in the following year Octavius Gilchrist had died. Among Clare's many friends and acquaintances in Stamford, Peterborough and the surrounding villages there were readers aplenty, but none possessed the worldly intelligence and understanding of the literary marketplace of Drury or Gilchrist's penetrating mind and profound knowledge of literature. Clare was, very much, on his own in trying to guess what the editors of the annuals might require.

The poem I want to concentrate on here is 'Ode to Autumn'. Like many of Clare's poems it has a complex history in manuscript, and I have no intention of trying to disentangle the various manuscript versions of the poem. It is not clear whether Clare intended this poem to be destined for an annual, probably not, but it is a poem to which he attached more than ordinary importance, and he made great efforts with it. In particular he enlisted the help of his London friend, Eliza Emmerson. By 1828 he had known Mrs Emmerson for eight years, and was not only grateful to her for her help in publicising his poems, but he had formed a justifiably high opinion of her intelligence and critical abilities. Having been sent a copy of 'Ode to Autumn' by Clare she wrote to him , with her customary enthusiasm, on 18 January 1828:

> And now, my gentle hearted Clare — what am I not to say in terms of admiration & thanks for your charming "Ode to Autumn" — my eyes have often revelled, & my heart feasted, on your pastoral measures — but, in <u>fair truth I tell you</u>, this "Ode" is by far the best, & choicest thing you have produced — it is well constructed — your <u>Images</u>, & <u>Epithets</u>, are admirably chosen, & beautifully supported thro' out the poem! How sweetly, & gracefully, have you embodied & given a personality to Autumn — who
> — "Oft at morning from her lattice peeps
> To beckon up the Sun!" — again you say —
> _ Sweet vision — with the wild deshevelled hair
> And raiments shadowy of each winds embrace" —
> The whole of the <u>3 last</u> Stanzas, are exquesitely beautiful, the <u>Image</u> and the <u>action</u> that supports the — "Wild Sorceress" — (oh what an

admirable epithet!) — She — who, "yet sublime o'er grief" &cc &cc,
is one of the most powerful, & poetic results of pastoral Song!
  "Soon must I mark thee as a pleasant dream" &cc &cc —
"Thy Life is waning now, & silence tries
    To mourn — thee — but meets no sympathy in Sounds —
    As stooping low she bends
      Forming with leaves thy grave
    To sleep inglorious there 'mid tangled woods
'Till parch'd lipped Summer pines in drought away
    Then, from thine Ivied trance
    Awake to glories new!"

If this — is not poesy & pathos, & symplicity, and originality, I
have no discrimination, or feeling, or taste in the composition of
the pastoral Ode! — you need not have told me "to shut out the
"Evening" of Collins" with all due respect to the harmony of his
flowing lines, &cc they were entirely obliterated, & "Evening" sunk
to quiet rest, the moment I conversed with your
    "Syren of sullen woods & fading hues" —.
I think — if you will pardon my suggestion) that the picture given
in your 6ᵗʰ Stanza might be more tender by saying — "We'll pillow
on the grass
      And fondly ruminate
    O'er the disorder'd scenes of woods & fields" —
This first, effort of your Muse in blank verse [   ] me, the most
conclusive proof, of what your Geni[us] may accomplish, in the
higher walks of Song[11]

She followed this letter with another a few days later, on 29 January
1828, which contained detailed suggestions:

My dear & kind Clare /
            Heaven be praised! if indeed the "dews" of sympathy
have so "refreshed" your mind & heart: In return, what sweet
insence have you not bestowed on me what "praises" have you not
lavished — aye, and I will hold them as sincerely offer'd, as were my
own "commendations" upon your "Ode to Autumn" — Perhaps,
by education I am not qualified to become the "Critic" — but, there
are perceptions of the true & beautiful which Learning never can
attain, & where its aid is quite unnecessary — Even such was my
case, in reading over your lovely Poem — fear not that I have viewed
it through the medium of a too partial judgment — No! I have
scrupulously sought out its little blemishes — some few words that
are harsh & inelegant to my ear, & some trifling grammatical errors
— I will tell you these now. — 1ˢᵗ Stanza, write haply for "aptly" — 2ᵈ

Stanza <u>foot</u> for "feet" -- <u>spreading</u> for "ramping" --- 3^d Stanza, <u>glossy</u> for "<u>Oily</u>" (I don't like <u>this</u> word in poesy!) -- 4th Stanza, <u>moaning</u>, or, running, "brook" -- instead of "crawling" -- for <u>liquid</u> <u>matter</u> <u>cannot crawl</u> -- 5th St^z -- (and oh, how beautiful it is!) first line write <u>so</u> "now" instead of "as now" -- <u>6th</u> St^{za} be it thus, if you please --
"Beneath the <u>twined</u> arms of this stunt Oak
<u>We'll</u> pillow on the grass,
And <u>fondly</u> ruminate
O'er the disordered scenes of woods & fields" - &cc &cc
9th Stanza, say, <u>weary</u> "with the din" -- "jostled" is a vulgar word -- 10th Stanza, is <u>all</u> <u>perfection</u>, in <u>thought</u> & <u>imagry</u>, and expressed in choice language! ------- 11th Stanza, do indulge me by saying <u>features</u> for "dresses" -- <u>haply</u> for "aptly" <u>this</u> stanza, forms a <u>sublime</u>, & <u>touching</u> <u>personification</u> of "Autumn". The last two stanzas are indeed beyond my praise --[12]

Clare studied these criticisms and suggestions carefully, and many he adopted. We don't have the version which Clare sent to Mrs Emmerson, but it seems to have originally begun;

Syren of sullen moods & fading hues
Yet aptly not incapable of joy
Sweet autumn I thee hail
With welcome all unfeigned

As we can see from the preceding letter, Mrs Emmerson didn't like 'aptly', which occurs again later in the poem, and Clare clearly agreed with her, changing the word, on both occasions, to 'haply' as she suggested. Similarly, the word 'oily' which she disliked was changed to 'glossy'. Even where Clare did not adopt the suggested alterations, he was prompted to think again and make alterations of his own.

It is at this point that Allan Cunningham enters the story. Cunningham was a Scot and an old friend of Clare's from their *London Magazine* days. They had met when Clare was in London and both men had attended the dinners which John Taylor and James Hessey had organised for contributors to their magazine. Cunningham and Clare found each other congenial company, partly because they were both men of working class origins who had become significant literary figures. Cunningham had been appointed editor of a new literary annual, to be called *The Anniversary*. This was to be a very superior annual. It was published by the bookseller John Sharpe and printed by Charles Whittingham of the Chiswick Press. Whittingham had established himself as one of the leading printers of the day and had collaborated with Sharpe over many years on a variety of projects. A number of their beautifully printed books are to be found in John Clare's library, for instance his 1826 edition of Goldsmith's poetry. *The Anniversary* was also to be larger than most of the other annuals, with the ordinary edition an octavo size at one guinea, rather than the 12 shillings which was the usual price for an annual, with a large paper edition as well, costing more.

Given the friendship between them, it is hardly surprising that Cunningham should ask Clare to contribute to his new annual. The 'Letters to John Clare' in the British Library do not contain any such request, so Cunningham must have asked Clare in person. Clare was in London in 1828 from late February to the end of March, staying with the Emmersons. It must have been during this period that Cunningham met Clare and asked for his help. Since Clare was staying with Mrs Emmerson, and given her admiration for the 'Ode to Autumn', it is hardly surprising that this is the poem which was sent to Cunningham. There was also the considerable advantage that there was a text of the poem in London, so Cunningham did not have to wait for Clare to return home and find a suitable poem among his manuscripts. Mrs Emmerson took the opportunity of sending a poem of her own, 'The Return', which Cunningham also printed in his annual, immediately after Clare's poem.

Cunningham acknowledged the receipt of the poems in a letter dated 20 March 1828, addressed to Clare at Mrs Emmerson's, shortly before he returned home:

My dear Clare,

Were I a true worldly minded Editor I should write you a letter of thanks very civil and very vague saying that your Ode to Autumn was very pretty and the ladys verses very fair. But I am not an Editor of that fashion—I only say what I think and feel – now listen. I think your ode one of the very happiest Poems you have written -- full of nature and truth and I think too that Mrs Emmersons "Return" has good feel good sense and good poetry.

I beg you will thank Mrs E. for me and assure her I feel the domestic truth of her verses. For yourself a more sordid reward awaits you on publication. In the meanwhile be assured I feel your kindness as well as I feel your verse and both are much after my own heart. [...]

I remain Dear Clare
Your very faithful friend
And fellow Bard Allan Cunningham[13]

The Anniversary was duly published in the late autumn of 1828, and was well received. It had a strong list of contributors, with several of Cunningham's fellow Scots — James Hogg, Thomas Pringle, John Wilson and J. G. Lockhart, as well as two poems by the editor himself. There was a posthumous contribution from Lord Byron as well as pieces from George Darley, Mary Russell Mitford, Agnes Strickland and Robert Southey. The illustrations, tellingly listed before the writings at the beginning of the volume, included engravings of paintings by Gainsborough, Turner, Landseer, Francis Danby and Sir Thomas Lawrence. It was, in every way, a most handsome volume. Cunningham wrote to Clare on 24 November 1828:

> My dear Clare
> Here is my little embellished Book what think you of it? It has been very favourably received and there can be little doubt of its future success if I can continue it in its commencing spirit. I enclose you Three sovereigns, and I am much obliged to you beside for your beautiful and very natural verses. I hope you will like the look of my book so much as will tempt you to write to me again. I need not say how much these books are looked at and how largely they affect ones name for good or evil. I beg you will pattle up your Muse in my behalf and give me one of those natural and glowing things which bring the hand to the lip. Tell me how you like my Book.
> I remain My dear Poet
> Yours ever faithfully
> Allan Cunningham[14]

Clare responded to Cunningham's request, and the latter replied on 6 April 1829: 'I have placed your contributions in the <u>approved</u> box marked with my hearty approbation.'[15] However, writing on 30 July 1829 Cunningham had unwelcome news: 'Alas for the Anniversary. It is sunk no more to rise and the proprieter has commenced a magazine in its stead. I am editor no longer but a plain simple man much at your service.'[16]

By the late 1820s many new annuals had started up, and competition was fierce; casualties were inevitable. In spite of its critical success, presumably the sales of *The Anniversary* were not sufficient to compensate for the expense involved in compiling the annual. The single issue which appeared remains one of the finest of all the literary annuals, both in terms of its contents and its presentation.

A century ago John Middleton Murry described 'Ode to Autumn' as Clare's 'most perfect poem'.[17] I suspect that not many readers would share that opinion today, but it certainly remains a very fine poem. It serves as an example of the untold stories which lie behind John Clare's poems, many of the stories more complicated than the one discussed here. It also gives us a good example of how Clare was always ready to use his friends to improve or advise on his poetry, rather than working in isolation; the reactions of others were always of importance to him. Here is the poem as it appeared in *The Anniversary*.

ODE TO AUTUMN.

BY JOHN CLARE.

SYREN! Of sullen woods and fading hues,
Yet haply not incapable of joy,---
    Sweet Autumn, I thee hail!
    With welcome all unfeigned;
And oft, as Morning from her lattice peeps.
To beckon up the Sun! I'll seek, with thee,
    To drink the dewy breath
    Of fields left fragrant then.
To solitudes, where no frequented path
But what thine own foot makes, betrays thine home,
    Stealing obtrusive there,
    To meditate thine end,
By overshadow'd ponds, in woody nooks,
With ramping sallows lined, and crowding sedge,
    That woo the winds to play,
    And with them dance for joy.

And meadow pools, torn wide by lawless floods,
Where waterlilies spread their glossy leaves,
    On which the dragon fly
    Yet battens in the sun;
Where leans the moping willow half way o'er,
On which the shepherd crawls astride, to throw
    His angle clear of weeds,
    That float the water's brim.

Or crispy hills, and hollows scant of sward,
Where, step by step, the patient shepherd boy
    Hath cut rude flights of stairs,

To climb their steepy sides;
Then, tracking at their feet, grown hoarse with noise,
The moaning brook, that ekes its weary speed,
And struggles through the weeds
With faint and sullen crawl.

These haunts, long favour'd, but the more so now,
With thee thus wandering, moralizing on;
Stealing glad thoughts from grief,
And happy though I sigh!
Sweet vision! with the wild dishevell'd hair,
And raiment shadowy with each wind's embrace,
Fain would I win thine harp
To one accordant theme.

Now, not inaptly craved, commencing thus:—
Beneath the twined arms of this stunt oak,
We'll pillow on the grass,
And fondly ruminate
O'er the disorder'd scenes of fields and woods,
Plough'd lands, thin travell'd by half hungry sheep;
Pastures track'd deep with cows,
Where small birds seek for seed.

Marking the cow boy—who so merry trills
His frequent unpremeditated song;
Wooing the winds to pause
'Till echo sings again,
As on, with plashy step and clouted shoon,
He roves, half indolent and self employ'd,
To rob the little birds
Of hips and pendent haws,

And sloes, dim cover'd, as with dewy veils,
And rambling brambleberries, pulp and sweet,
Arching their prickly trails
Half o'er the narrow lane;
And mark the hedger, front with stubborn face
The dank rude wind, that whistles thinly by,
His leathern garb, thorn proof,
And cheeks red hot with toil!

Wild sorceress! me thy restless mood delights
More than the stir of summer's crowded scenes;
Where, giddy with the din,

Joy pall'd mine ear with song:
Heart sickening for the silence that is thine—
    That lone and vagrant bee
    Roams faint with weary chime.

The filtering winds, that winnow through the woods
In tremulous noise, now bid, at ev'ry breath,
    Some sickly canker'd leaf
    Let go its hold and die!
And now the bickering storm, with sudden start,
In fitful gusts of anger carpeth loud;
    Thee urging to thine end,
    Sore wept by troubled skies!

And yet, sublime in grief, thy thoughts delight
To show me visions of more gorgeous dyes:
    Haply forgetting now,
    They but prepare thy shroud!
Thy pencil, dashing its excess of shades,
Improvident of waste, 'till every bough
    Burns with thy mellow touch,
    Disorderly divine!

Soon must I view thee as a pleasant dream,
Droop faintly, and so sicken for thine end,
    As sad the winds sink low,
    In dirges for their queen!
While in the moment of their weary pause,
To cheer thy bankrupt pomp, the willing lark
    Starts from his shielding clod,
    Snatching sweet scraps of song!

Thy life is waning now, and Silence tries
To mourn, but meets no sympathy in sounds,
    As stooping low she bends,
    Forming with leaves thy grave!
To sleep inglorious there 'mid tangled woods,
'Till parch-lipp'd Summer pines in drought away—
    Then from thine ivy'd trance
    Awake to glories new.

NOTES

For permission to quote from the 'Letters to John Clare' I must thank the Manuscript Department of the British Library.

1   David Stewart has recently challenged the commonly held view that the market for single-author volumes of poetry largely disappeared in the 1820s, in *The Form of Poetry in the 1820s and 1830s: A Period of Doubt* (London: Palgrave, 2018).

2   Frederick W. Faxon, *Literary Annuals and Gift Books: A Bibliography, 1823-1903* (Pinner: Private Libraries Association, 1973).

3   Andrew Boyle, *An Index to the Annuals, Vol. 1: The Authors (1820-1850)* (Worcester: Andrew Boyle Ltd., 1967).

4   Harry Hootman, *British Literary Annuals and Giftbooks 1823-1861*, unpublished doctoral thesis, University of South Carolina, 2004.

5   Katherine D. Harris, *Forget Me Not: The Rise of the British Literary Annual, 1823-1835* (Athens, Ohio: Ohio University Press, 2015).

6   James Hogg, *Contributions to Annuals and Gift-Books* (Edinburgh: Edinburgh University Press, 2006).

7   The precise number depends on what, exactly, one considers to be an annual, a question discussed in detail by Harris in *Forget Me Not*; she attributes thirty-nine poems to Clare.

8   Eleanore Jamieson, 'The Binding Styles of the Gift Books and Annuals' in the 1973 reprint of Faxon.

9   David Stewart, *The Form of Poetry*, p. 71.

10 British Library Egerton Manuscript (hereafter Eg.) 2248, fol. 186^r; Louis Theodore Ventouillac had arrived in this country from his native France in 1816 and established himself as an editor and author; presumably he was assisting Dale with the editing of this annual.

11 Eg. 2247, fols 393^v-94^r.

12 Eg. 2247, fols 397^{r-v}.

13 Eg. 2247, fol.422^r.

14 Eg. 2248, fol. 80^r.

15 Eg. 2248, fol. 133^r.

16 Eg. 2248, fol. 161^r.

17 *Times Literary Supplement*, 13 January 1921, p. 17, in a review of *John Clare: Poems: Chiefly from Manuscript*, ed. by Edmund Blunden and Alan Porter (1920).

'The Herdsman's Cottage, or Sunset', Samuel Palmer, 1850, etching.
Metropolitan Museum of Art, New York.

Reviews

The Ballad-Singer in Georgian and Victorian London. By OSKAR COX JENSEN. Cambridge: Cambridge University Press. 2021. Pp. xviii + 280. £75.

The ballad-singer is an enigmatic figure in British culture. In recent years, scholarship has tended to focus on the surviving physical resources that pertain to the art of ballad-singing. Analyses of lyrics and their narrative content have been conducted, often in conjunction with contextual investigations into the material and print histories of broadside ballads and song sheets. It is safe to say that we now know far more about the songs (in printed form) than we do about the singers who might have sung them. In *The Ballad-Singer in Georgian and Victorian London*, Oskar Cox Jensen sets out to address this imbalance, and provide some insights into the social and cultural history of the ballad-singer during the late-eighteenth and nineteenth centuries.

The monograph is divided into four main chapters that attempt to illuminate some characteristics of the life and work of the ballad-singer – an undertaking that is, incidentally, beautifully represented on the book's cover which features Henry Robert Morland's striking painting of a candlelit singer looming out of the darkness. The first chapter focuses primarily on visual representations of the ballad-singer; the second chapter considers the ballad-singer's position in relation to narratives of national progress and improvement as presented in textual sources and movement through the city; the third chapter looks at the 'geographic, sonic, (and) social' (19) challenges of performance faced by the ballad-singer; and the last chapter explores the repertoire of these singers. This outline gives a sense of the interdisciplinary breadth of Cox Jensen's study. While largely successful, there are a few moments where analysis of the comparisons drawn by writers and artists between ballad-singers and other members of society would benefit from more thorough investigation: the discussion of the respective agency of ballad-singers and sex workers being a case in point. Between chapters, the writer includes 'Interludes' which take a ballad as a worked example of themes addressed in the preceding chapter, and as a 'stepping stone' (17) towards the next chapter. These structural decisions are innovative and engaging, playfully imitating the structure of some ballads to some extent, and do serve their purpose of providing a greater coherence to the study's wide-ranging themes. Nevertheless, the use of songs in these interludes as a lens through which to see the singer sometimes relegates the ballad-singer to the background, thereby reinforcing the fact that scholarship has been, and continues to be, weighted towards the songs and not the singers.

Cox Jensen makes the case that ballad-singers 'fulfilled a vital and significant historical role: in mediating the musical mainstream, in disseminating news and opinion, in the construction of communities both local and national' (247). Moreover, Cox Jensen's use of primary sources and case studies dispel the 'false collectivity' (23) of ballad-singers as a homogenous

'Bridge and Cows', from *Liber Studiorum,* I, plate 2, designed and etched
by Joseph Mallord William Turner, engraved by Charles Turner, 1807.
Metropolitan Museum of Art, New York.

group. On these points, the writer's
arguments are particularly compelling,
well-researched and original. The
ballad recordings that accompany the
book and which are accessible online
through the publisher's website are not
only innovative, but also help ground
the academic writing in its real-world
context; this is, of course, a study of the
phenomenon of song, which could never
be fully articulated on the page alone.

Perhaps as a result of the many
different dimensions of the ballad-
singer that are mediated by Cox
Jensen, the spatial and temporal
parameters of the book are fixed on
London during the eighteenth and
nineteenth centuries. While such
delimitations are necessary to create

a coherent stand-alone volume, the
justifications for such decisions in *The
Ballad-Singer* are sometimes awkward.
For instance, in relation to ballad-
singing – but applicable to almost
anything one might care to think
about – the unsubstantiated claim
that 'things not only happened first in
London, they happened *more*' (10) is
largely unknowable at best, and deeply
problematic at worst. Similarly, while
the writer's attention to the London
ballad-singer within the specified time
period is well-sourced and evidenced,
very little is communicated about
the circumstances of the ballad-
singer leading up to or after this
time. The nineteenth-century ballad-
singer is framed as an anachronistic

102

Elizabethan throw-back (2) and compared to 'the fool of a medieval court' (82), but more could have been made of these comparisons and what they say about the changing socio-cultural role of (song-) performance over time. On another occasion, ballad-singing is expressed in terms of a 'tradition' (82) which is, frustratingly, not defined or elaborated further. As a result, opportunities to discuss, or even gesture towards, other ballad-singing individuals, the period's singing poets like William Blake and John Clare, for example, are not taken up.

At the other end of the book's time scale, Cox Jensen concludes his work by describing how the ballad-singer was all but killed off in the late nineteenth century by a more musically proficient population, a profusion of 'sonic and musical vibrancy (and) increased literacy' (247). The writer successfully shows how and why this might be true of the London-centric ballad-singer at the heart of this publication – but it could be made clearer that their experience was not necessarily shared by all ballad-singers, especially those located elsewhere. While heralding the extinction of the London ballad-singer allows this book to come to a neat conclusion, an acknowledgement of the myriad of different contexts wherein ballad-singing continued (and continues) to be a powerful form of individual and collective expression might have been a more successful means of reclaiming the ballad-singer from obscurity.

Nevertheless, Cox Jensen's monograph is an eloquent and most welcome addition to scholarship of the practice of folk song and street music. It has succeeded in illuminating many characteristics of the London ballad-singer that warrant closer attention and further research. Ambitious in its scope and innovative in its method and structure, *The Ballad-Singer* is an important academic work, but it is also an engaging socio-cultural history of human life that would be enjoyed by anyone interested in music and song.

John Blackmore
University of Exeter and
University of Bristol

Palgrave Advances in John Clare Studies. Edited by SIMON KÖVESI and ERIN LAFFORD. London: Palgrave Macmillan. 2020. Pp. xvii + 317. £24.99.

Palgrave Advances in John Clare Studies demonstrates an impressive range of judicious and distinct approaches to Clare's poetry. This well-balanced collection fits with a trend in twenty-first-century scholarship, in that it seeks to assert Clare's agency and complicate the long-held perspective of him as a lonely figure defined by what he lacked, rather than what he had. As the editors assert, 'for all his awkwardness, Clare's was a sociability that operated in a wide variety of circumstances and social settings' (4), and this 'sociability' is drawn out through essays that uncover the rich cross-cultural links in his work.

The Clare that emerges from these pages is determined and innovative, adaptable to literary tastes, even business-like in his publishing dealings. David Stewart presents a poet attuned to 'a changing and highly diverse poetic scene' (18) in the 1820s and 30s, and prepared to fit his work according to the tastes of the annuals and magazines which published his work. Clare, as a result, participates in a 'creative self-fashioning' (21) that runs against more precious notions of 'authenticity'; indeed, toying with notions of authenticity is part of the wider theatrical play that is evident in his poetry.

Clare's artistic ambitions are also demonstrated in the chapters on music. Kirsteen McCue and Stephanie Kuduk Weiner build upon the work of George Deacon and others on the importance of folk songs to an understanding of his work. McCue looks at Clare's spells of song-writing activity, which resulted in several poems being set to music in concert halls and drawing rooms, as well as the missed opportunities, such as his abandoned English 'national and provincial' song project. Weiner considers Clare's transcripts and imitations of vernacular song, spanning the influences of commercial, folk and church music. Clare, she notes, participated in 'a living song tradition' (66), and 'never stopped writing songs for his readers to sing' (73).

Sara Lodge and Andrew Hodgson's chapters are closer readings of the poetry that point to Clare's metrical and rhythmic skill. Lodge compellingly considers his experimentation with literary forms, which she configures as 'landforms', 'because they attend and attune themselves so closely to the shapes and rhythms of the natural world, and to their expression in dialect and the patterns of rural life' (89). This formulation leads to a reworked, broader idea of his famed 'sense of place', encompassing the influence, for example, of Scots dialect. Clare artfully plays with the expected regularity of forms, and Lodge draws links between the line and the land, the idea of the 'open and closed' landscapes and forms (101), while developing a persuasive theory of Clare's 'waywardness' – 'a directed openness to paths that become

the lines that feet may take' (106). Hodgson, in a series of expert readings, detects the productive interplay of spontaneity and artifice in Clare's ballad forms. Commendably, he draws links to the asylum verse, where unsteady rhythms are used to evoke hesitation, loss of direction, and alienation.

There is a 'waywardness', too, in the restless, animating tensions when Clare writes about animal movement – the focus of James Castell's study. Castell's engaging analysis develops the ecocritical approach to Clare, where the poet's animals are not simply rooted in place, but demonstrate agility and agency in straying beyond the bounds of their dwellings. Again, we are being invited to reconfigure the long-valued 'sense of place' in these works. Other chapters, too, draw upon notions of community established between human and animal. Katey Castellano presents a perspective on the bird nesting poems that models the improvisational work of wild animals upon private land as 'continuing the work of communing after enclosure'. Thus human and animal might share wild sovereignty, in opposition to the encroachment of private property; free-flowing birdsong, in itself, resists the boundaries of time and space drawn up by capitalism. Scott Hess, in the most theoretically weighty of these essays, reads Clare as an early poet of 'the posthuman', where the centrality of the human is challenged, and multiple subjectivities and perspectives proliferate. In these environments, the idea of a single form of 'knowing' is complicated, and feelings of surprise, shock and wonder proliferate. Michael Nicholson considers how Clare reconciles different dimensions of 'stress' in his poetry, drawing upon links to other writers such as Stephen

Duck, William Cobbett and James Thomson, and outlining how Clare's 'lyric sensitivity to distress' enables an openness to both human and non-human communities.

The Shepherd's Calendar is a work that deserves continued critical attention, and Sara Houghton-Walker's enjoyable essay outlines a range of productive dynamics in the poem: the specific versus the general, the linear versus the circular, and the overarching motif of constancy and change. With a particular focus on 'November', Houghton-Walker explores the self-consciousness of Clare's shepherd – both a specific and general figure, positioned at once as poetic subject and observer. This 'complicating distance' (148) allows Clare's sophistication to flourish, producing a work that is neither quite lyric nor narrative in form, problematising the ability to 'know' his subject matter – as he acknowledges the sense of distance that is necessary to write, but which alienates the self from the community (a similar analytical approach might be taken to some of Clare's earlier work, most notably Lubin in 'The Village Minstrel').

The collection concludes with two provocative and valuable pieces on Clare's later work. Erin Lafford's highly original reading of Clare focuses on the idea of hypochondria – 'as a social and literary culture that Clare wanted to participate in (...) and as a form of poetic imagination and attention'. Through this approach, Lafford cautions us not to see Clare simply as a poet of 'immediacy' but also as one who exhibits moments of imaginative fancy – even 'hypochondriac fancy'. James Whitehead's concluding chapter makes the vital claim that we should seek to dissolve the barrier between Clare's early and later writing, and take a more integrated critical approach. Casting further light on the asylum period, he provides deserved focus on the role of William Knight, steward at Northampton Asylum, and asks us to consider the cultural influences that permeated even into Victorian asylums (while never misleading us into thinking of these as 'happy' places). As this entire book demonstrates, a critical focus on 'community' and 'sociability' yields diverse, engaging and fruitful readings of Clare's work. Whitehead's challenge is that we extend the same rigorous critical frames to his asylum verse – an appealing and important idea for Clare scholarship to come.

Thomas Williams

Stories of Trees, Woods, and the Forest. Edited by FIONA STAFFORD. Everyman's Pocket Classics. New York, London, Toronto: Alfred A. Knopf. 2021. Pp. 479. £12.99.

Some of the stories in the Everyman's Pocket Classics anthology *Stories of Trees, Woods, and the Forest* feature charismatic individual trees: an apple tree bearing a strange resemblance to a dead woman haunts the husband who resented her; a pear tree's cluster of blossoms consolidates its steward's feelings of happiness, hope, and loss; a local act of Maori anti-colonial resistance coalesces around a threatened totara tree. Others focus on the forest as an indeterminate collective, whether it is the scene of 'sylvan liberty' (333) for Thomas Love Peacock's Robin Hood and Maid Marian, or the fold of danger which closes upon Angela Carter's Red Riding Hood 'like a pair of jaws.' (354)

Fiona Stafford has assembled a beautiful selection of arboreal short stories and excerpts from around the world and from different periods of literary history, including several representatives of the Romantic period. Ovid, Jane Austen, Tove Jansson, R. K. Narayan, and a range of others are placed in fruitful and revealing conversation. An impressive variety of genres – myth, fairy tale, fable, romance, horror, mystery, psychological drama, social comedy – are brought together under one leafy canopy.

One of the gratifications of collections like these is their capacity to redirect attention to themes or settings that might otherwise go unnoticed. As Stafford observes in the introduction, while many of these stories overtly centre trees or woods, in others 'trees seem little more than a passing detail, but they have a tendency to grow between the lines' (13). The stories which become, often surprisingly, 'stories of trees' by virtue of their inclusion in the collection are some of the most rewarding. Washington Irving's 'The Legend of Sleepy Hollow', for example, one of the longer stories in the anthology, has its centre of gravity shifted from the famous phantom headless horseman to a character which many readers probably overlook: 'an enormous tulip-tree' (61) whose white lightning scar appears like a hanging shroud. What does it mean to read familiar and unfamiliar tales through their trees' branches? A single sentence in an extract from Stella Gibbons' *Cold Comfort Farm* takes on tremendous moment when it appears in the middle of this book: 'Flora used sometimes to ask him the name of a tree, but he never knew.' (186)

Readers of *Stories of Trees, Woods, and the Forest* will not come to know trees. These trees and forests are cryptic, weird, and repeatedly misread or misused. They are strikingly withdrawn, even when front and centre or all-surrounding. Yet they are remarkably generous too, in the emotional, psychological, and aesthetic work that they can do. This is a book about how people feel about trees, whether those feelings are concentrated upon a single specimen or more nebulously associated with the wild wood, or even when characters and narrators don't realise that they're responding to the forest around them at all. As well as the loveliness of its individual stories, this anthology offers a wider view of the literary abundance of trees.

Tess Somervell
Worcester College,
University of Oxford

Melodys of Earth and Sky. By JULIAN PHILIPS. NMC recordings. Available on CD and streaming platforms. 2022. £12.99.

Clare's relationship with music is currently a critical staple in assessing the poet. Over two hundred tunes appear in his notebooks, some learned by ear from fellow travellers and others copied from books for him to play back on his fiddle. George Deacon's influential *John Clare and the Folk Tradition* (1983) offers a scholarly introduction to the rural community of which Clare was an active member, and connects the folk traditions and customs of Helpston and Northamptonshire to his poetry, letters, notes, and music. *Melodys of Earth and Sky* follows in this tradition by presenting nine creative transcriptions from Clare's books of fiddle tunes reimagined by the composer Julian Philips for clarinet and violin. The tunes alternate with a series of narrations of Clare's writings by Toby Jones, who also played Clare in Andrew Kötting and Iain Sinclair's film, *By Our Selves* (2014). While Jones' sonorous readings of poems like 'Song's Eternity' and 'First Love' and prose extracts 'The edge of the orison' and 'On Gypsies' are compelling, Philips' project here is to connect the listener with Clare the musician. Jones' words lightly echo through Philips' stark, clean, but always clement tunes, evocative as they are of a folk tradition at once political, domestic, and felicitous. As we read in the introductory note to the album: 'It is hoped that this offers the listener a rich experience of Clare's remarkable creative legacy as a poet and musician, and its extraordinary and urgent resonance in our troubled age of pandemic, climate catastrophe, technological alienation and political instability'. The introduction, like the excellent sleeve notes on the music and fully reproduced texts, is guided by Clare expert, Simon Kövesi, consultant to the project and originator of the words and music event from which the album emerged. The event, planned for April 2020 to mark the bicentenary of Clare's *Poems Descriptive of Rural Life and Scenery*, was cancelled during the first COVID lockdown, but its intention – to reimagine Clare's poetry through sound and song – evolved into this recording.

The sometimes haunting and stark resonances of Kate Romano's clarinet and Ionel Manciu's violin befits the unusual time of their inception: the lockdown context grants an intimacy and strangeness to the instrumental melodies that would perhaps be missing if recorded today. What we are left with is a listening experience into which we are hospitably invited, one that recalls the merriment Clare felt with the gypsy fiddlers and fortune tellers from whom he learned his trade and with whom he drank and danced. But it also entangles us in the environment in which Clare was immersed, visually depicted by Brian Shield's striking cover art of the poet recumbent amidst the undergrowth and listening intently to a nightingale. In Shield's depiction, Clare is masked like a Venetian *Medico della peste*, his long golden beak and angelic brown wings a carnivalesque allusion to the singing nightingale at his side. A plague doctor for our own times, Clare offers the listener a melodic salve, one beautifully celebrated in this sequence of songs.

Emma Mason
University of Warwick

Detail, 'History of a Coat',
Glasgow Looking Glass,
4 (23 July 1825).

Contributors

ALEX BROADHEAD is Lecturer in English Language and Literature at the University of Liverpool, and his interests lie in the area of dialect in eighteenth- and nineteenth-century literature. Linguistic creativity is a recurring focus of his work, which employs the tools of stylistics and sociolinguistics to illustrate how, for many of the writers of this period, dialect was a source of joyful experimentation. He has published on Wordsworth, Josiah Relph and (with Jane Hodson) Romantic-era fiction. His first monograph, *The Language of Robert Burns: Style, Ideology and Identity*, was published in 2014, and he has another in preparation, on the language of early dialect literature. His contribution to this year's *JCSJ* develops some of the ideas introduced in his article for the 2021 issue, titled 'John Clare and the Northamptonshire dialect: rethinking language and place'.

MOINAK CHOUDHURY is a PhD Candidate at the University of Minnesota, Twin Cities. His current research examines narratives of popular politics in the long eighteenth century by looking at the figure of the autodidact. Moinak's articles on relations between space, place, and populace have appeared in *The Cultural Heritage of Sikkim* (Routledge, 2018) and trade publications in India. He is also collaborating on a digital humanities project mapping captivity in Britain and North Africa.

ROBERT HEYES is an inorganic chemist by training, a school teacher by profession, and a book collector by inclination. Unlike some collectors he likes to make use of his books, rather than just sit and admire the display they make on the shelves (although he does that as well). Over the years he has done a good deal of research on John Clare, with a particular emphasis on Clare's letters, and those of his friends and associates. He is currently carrying out research on Clare's activities as a naturalist.

BRIDGET KEEGAN is a Professor of English and Dean of Arts and Sciences at Creighton University in Omaha, Nebraska. She has published extensively on eighteenth-century and Romantic-period poetry. Her books include a volume of *Eighteenth-Century English Labouring-Class Poets* (2003), *British Labouring-Class Nature Poetry, 1730–1837* (2008), and *The Eighteenth-Century Literature Handbook* (2009). Most recently she is the co-editor, with John Goodridge, of Cambridge University Press's *A History of British Working-Class Literature* (2017).

KAZUTAKE KITA is an Associate Professor in Liberal Arts at Tokyo University of Science, Japan. His interests as an applied linguist cover diverse areas including corpus linguistics, critical discourse analysis, English language teaching, and stylistics. He has published essays on a variety of topics, among which is John Clare's sonnet writing. He is the Japanese translator of *The Smartest Kids in the World: And How They Got That Way* by Amanda Ripley (Simon & Schuster, 2013), and also a Japanese co-translator of *Translation in Language Teaching: An Argument for Reassessment* by Guy Cook (Oxford University Press, 2010).

EMMA NUDING is a Doctoral Fellow at the Centre for Medieval Studies, University of York. Her PhD thesis charts the reception of St Guthlac of Crowland from the medieval period to the present, covering texts in Old English, Middle English and Latin, as well modern novels and poetry. She is particularly interested in how the features of fenland landscapes actively shape fenland writing, and also in how medieval texts shape modern ones. Her wider research interests include ecocriticism, gender, sexuality, and pilgrimage. Both as a teacher and as a researcher, Emma is committed to widening access to medieval culture.

Abbreviations

BIOGRAPHY *John Clare, A Biography,* Jonathan Bate (London: Picador, 2003)

BY HIMSELF *John Clare By Himself,* ed. Eric Robinson and David Powell (Ashington and Manchester: Mid-NAG and Carcanet, 1996)

COTTAGE TALES *John Clare, Cottage Tales,* ed. Eric Robinson, David Powell and P.M.S. Dawson (Ashington and Manchester: Mid-NAG and Carcanet, 1993)

CRITICAL HERITAGE *Clare: The Critical Heritage,* ed. Mark Storey (London: Routledge & Kegan Paul, 1973)

EARLY POEMS (I–II) *The Early Poems of John Clare,* ed. Eric Robinson, David Powell and Margaret Grainger (Oxford: Clarendon Press, 1989)

JOHN CLARE IN CONTEXT, ed. Hugh Haughton, Adam Phillips and Geoffrey Summerfield (Cambridge: Cambridge University Press, 1994)

JCSJ *The John Clare Society Journal* (1982–)

LATER POEMS *The Later Poems of John Clare,* ed. Eric Robinson, David Powell and Margaret Grainger (Oxford: Clarendon Press, 1984)

LETTERS *The Letters of John Clare,* ed. Mark Storey (Oxford: Clarendon Press, 1985)

MIDDLE PERIOD (I–II) *John Clare, Poems of the Middle Period 1822–1837,* ed. Eric Robinson, David Powell and P.M.S. Dawson (Oxford: Clarendon Press, 1996); (III–IV) (1998); (V) (2003)

MIDSUMMER CUSHION *John Clare, The Midsummer Cushion,* ed. Kelsey Thornton and Anne Tibble (Ashington and Manchester: Mid-NAG and Carcanet, revised edition, 1990)

NATURAL HISTORY *The Natural History Prose Writings of John Clare,* ed. Margaret Grainger (Oxford: Clarendon Press, 1983)

NEW APPROACHES *John Clare, New Approaches,* ed. John Goodridge and Simon Kövesi (Helpston: John Clare Society, 2000)

NORTHBOROUGH SONNETS *John Clare, Northborough Sonnets,* ed. Eric Robinson, David Powell and P.M.S. Dawson (Ashington and Manchester: Mid-NAG and Carcanet, 1995)

PROSE *The Prose of John Clare,* ed. J.W. and Anne Tibble (London: Routledge & Kegan Paul, 1951, reprinted 1970)

SHEPHERD'S CALENDAR *John Clare, The Shepherd's Calendar,* ed. Eric Robinson, Geoffrey Summerfield and David Powell (Oxford: Oxford University Press, revised edition, 1993)